HIVE

HIVE

THE SIMPLE GUIDE
TO MULTIGENERATIONAL LIVING

HOW OUR FAMILY MAKES IT WORK

LISA M. CINI

HIVE
THE SIMPLE GUIDE TO MULTIGENERATIONAL LIVING

iUniverse books may be ordered through booksellers or by contacting:

iUniverse
1663 Liberty Drive
Bloomington, IN 47403
www.iuniverse.com
1-800-Authors (1-800-288-4677)

ISBN: 978-1-5320-2063-6 (sc)
ISBN: 978-1-5320-2065-0 (hc)
ISBN: 978-1-5320-2064-3 (e)

Print information available on the last page.

iUniverse rev. date: 06/20/2017

CONTENTS

Field Notes

DEDICATION

This book is dedicated to My Hive:

Great Grandma Gerline Lilly
John Miller
Elizabeth (Libby) Miller
Greg Cini
Jacob Cini
Adellina Cini
Callie Cini (the dog)
The Bees, too many to mention by name ☺
Rapunzel (RIP), Snow White, Jasmine, Belle,
Pocahontas & Cruella (AKA the chickens)
&
Piglet and Eeyore (the bunnies)

Matthew John Miller – Little Matt
548 Forever in our hearts and on our minds

INTRODUCTION: THE HIVE

Behind the idea for this book is my hope that anyone who picks it up and reads it will see an opportunity to connect, and care for, their family—all different ages of their family—under one roof. This idea is not new; my family just went back to what worked many years ago.

It's very important to me that this book adds great value and insight to your life. I think of it as "cafeteria style." Pick what you like, turn to which chapter you need. Take what's valuable and enjoy the meal. Please try not to bite off more than you can chew, not in this book, nor in the idea behind it: Multi-generational living as a positive way to live with your family…your kids, grandparents and great-parents, if you're fortunate enough to have them with you.

Here's how we designed the book to work for you. The beginning section, which we call "Parkview", explains the tangible design decisions behind the whats, whys, and hows of our 4-Generational living experiment. This is your guide for setting up your own multi-generational family situation. Nothing is meant to be taken as an absolute; it's just the way it works for us. Think of it as a recipe, you can always change it up. Everyone makes their pizza differently, this is our Cini Family Pizza recipe.

Next, you'll see the section we named, How to Stay Alive in the Hive. In our social experiment, we've figured out some things that help us move forward, better and stronger. In this way, I see our living arrangement being much like a beehive, where the bees all have their unique purpose that contributes to a better, stronger hive.

Sometimes, in our hive, we figured them out just through dumb luck, and sometimes through planning, and sometimes through pain. But it always was, and always will be, "an experiment" and just like taking a walk in the woods, we learned "which berries we could eat and which we couldn't." The good news is…no one's starved and the better news is everyone's thriving.

Finally, you'll find the section we call, Field Notes. If you were to stop by one day and visit us at our house, and sit around our dining room table, hang out together in our family room, spend a little time with Grandma (and Great-Grandma) Lilly, these are some things you might observe. They're the sweet things and the challenging things, the funny things and poignant things that really are the inner workings of our family.

We're learning as we're living. If you're thinking of starting your own social experiment, these strategies are here to help start you out on more solid ground than we did, but our hope is you'll see it as your own social experiment, and you'll create your own design for thriving in your own hive.

CHAPTER 1

WHO WE ARE

My family history is a mix of immigrants.

Our roots run as far back as the first American settlers, on my French-English side, to the turn of the 20th century, on my Irish-Italian-German-Jewish side. Yet, as far apart and dissimilar as our sides might seem, there's one thing that that ties us together: the bond to family.

I was taught, by all sides, that you should give more than you get, and while this started with family, it expanded outward to include neighbors, and then, country. Some might see this as an obligation, one that is heavy and often hard to bear, but I don't. I believe that one of the greatest gifts my ancestors gave me was a passion to put family first. Growing up, I heard stories about what this meant to the earlier generations, and sometimes, I saw it clearly, myself.

In Canton, Ohio. Sunday dinners were hosted by my paternal Italian grandmother.

Regardless of the economics of the time, her table was always full of food and people. All were welcome, and all showed up: cousins, friends, borders from the past, as well as the present. I heard that none of that changed much, when, even in midst of the Depression, my great-grandparents, Antonio and Assunta DeCosmo, shared all they had with their neighbors, so no one would suffer.

In southern West Virginia, close to the New River, my maternal grandparents lived on top of Hix Mountain and had their own orchards and gardens. "Extreme hospitality" sounds like it could be the name of a reality TV show, but it was actually my grandparents, John and Gerline Lilly's manner of living. Their table was always full of wonderful food, and their door was always open to anyone passing through. Just as in my Italian grandmother's home, here too, it was a high offense not to eat what was given. The only difference? Grandma Della (Assunta's daughter) offered pizza as an appetizer, dandelion greens salad, sautéed green, red and yellow peppers and sausage, spaghetti, and sliced oranges with olive oil and pepper. Compared to Grandma Lilly's offering of meatloaf, fresh green beans, white beans with corn bread, loaded with butter, made in a cast iron skillet, and pies of every possible variety.

Though food was a large part of what it meant to care for someone, or show your love, it didn't stop there. You could always count on having more attention being lavished on you as guest in either of their homes than at a 5-Star resort hotel. Should you find yourself sick, you'd receive better treatment than if you were in the intensive care unit at a major hospital. And though I was grateful to be nursed back, not just to *full* health, but to *perfect* health, part of me always feared what seemed to be the very real possibility of smothering to death under the weight of heavy wool blankets, or drowning to death by a third, necessary, cup of tea.

Growing up I thought this was all quite normal, and understood that loving each other meant supporting each other…in whatever way was needed.

So when I started my business 18 years ago and my daughter, Adellina, was ill, I didn't hesitate to ask my mother to move to Columbus to help. It was ideal, as it would provide a house for them to live in for as long as they desired. The kids would grow, and need less and less help, which was a perfect plan, because as my parents aged, they'd probably be able to help less. Not only would they not have to worry about what they could, or could not, afford to move into after my father retired, the house had room for family to visit comfortably.

She accepted our offer, and two years later, after my father retired, he followed; during those two years he drove the two hours down from Canton every weekend to be with my mother. It was the ideal exchange, as she could help with my kids, and have room for the rest of the grandkids around when they'd come from all around: Kentucky, Las Vegas, and other parts of Ohio. There were summers when my mother would pack up the kids and drive them down to West Virginia to see her parents, my kids' great-grandparents, while other summers saw her heading out with them to Las Vegas to visit my sister who lived there.

But as innovative an idea as this may sound, it really wasn't. When my father's parents could no longer function at home by themselves, they'd rotate among their four kids' homes. My grandparents enjoyed living this way right up until their last two years of life, when, at 98 and nearly 100 years old, they moved into an "Assisted Living" home. But for them, and their families, "assisted living" was really what they had been doing all those years.

Seeing everyone in the family always pitching in to help each other out, seeing multiple generations together, this was all normal for me, and so in the back of my mind I always had a Master Plan, and with my parents living in a house nearby, Phase One was officially up and running.

In 2004, my grandfather John Lilly, a former West Virginia coal miner, got black lung disease. The decision was made to sell the farm on the mountaintop, the one with the beautiful orchards and gardens, and move in with my parents in Columbus. Every morning, my children would go to my parents' house and would have breakfast with their grandparents and great grandparents. Is that normal? For my kids it was. And when my grandfather passed after 3 months, my grandmother continued to live with my parents.

The years went by and things went on this way, trouble-free.

But as with every good story, this plot had a twist, and it can be described in one word: *Grandma*. First she turned 91, then 92. She was living with my mother and father (see the pattern?) and one day it suddenly dawned on me, *Grandma could live to 99, or 100, just like my other grandparents! And what on earth would happen if she did? And moreover…what on earth would we do if she did?*

Maybe you're wondering what kind of monster I am to be so callous? But the exact opposite is true; I adore my grandmother. Growing up, some of my best memories are of us traveling to visit her in West Virginia. Once there, she always made the best food, always let us explore and be independent adventurers in a beautiful land—of course "independent" meant gourmet lunches packed for us all. She loved us and she showed it, and I was beginning to realize that soon it would be my turn to do the same for her. How soon was soon? That, I didn't know yet.

I was raised in a family with faith; it was a family where longevity was the norm and a sense of humor was a necessary part of survival. When our Great Aunts, Uncles, Grandparents died, there was sadness, but also lots of great stories, and always an appreciation that they lived, not just a long life, but it was a *quality* life. Translation: they weren't wasting away by themselves in the "*home*." With Grandma, while I didn't want her to take that ride on the "celestial elevator," I knew that when she did, she would not be sad. She had lived and loved well. She had faith, and she desired to be with my grandfather again. But she was still going strong into her 90s and that created our plot twist.

Phase Two of my Master Plan had always been the following: when my parents' home became too much of a burden, sell it and move them in with us. Lately, it seemed like we were getting very close to rolling out Phase Two. I'd already started noticing my parents and grandmother, struggling to handle their 4 bedroom, 3 bath home. Struggling with its full front and back yards, struggling with its mother-in-law suite. And while they loved the house, and their neighbors, eventually, the struggles became too great.

Phase Two was viable because of my life's work. I'd been Director of Interior Design at a leading and award winning, Senior Living company in the United States. Now I owned my own award winning interior design firm, and one of our areas of specialization was Senior Living. Additionally, I wrote and spoke on the subject of Dementia and Alzheimer's design.

However, Phase Two had a specific snag: our house was a four-story box. A French Manor house that was on the National Historic Register, which we loved and that worked beautifully for the four of us. But for it to work for all 3 generations would require an elevator. I had even researched putting one in for my parents. Unfortunately, even with an elevator, it would not be feasible to have all 4-Generations living under this home's mansard roof.

There was another solution, a little more complicated, perhaps, but a solution nonetheless. And so I started looking for another house, one that would serve all of our many and diverse needs. It had to have enough room for four generations and enough space for my son and daughter to spend their high school years, with as many friends over as needed and with all of them feeling welcome and loved. This was saying a lot since both Jacob and Adellina were on soccer teams, and Jacob was in the drum line, and Adellina in the choir, and they both were leaders in Young Life. The house needing to accommodate 20-40 kids in the home at any given time was a real possibility.

The hunt was on, and one night I saw the perfect house. It wasn't far from where we were living, so the kids would have a smooth transition, and the yard was like a national park. Though there had already been several additions to the house, there was no mother-in-law suite, and so a renovation would be required. That was fine, we'd be able to handle that. Things moved fast: we bought the house, put ours up for sale, and later put my parents'/grandmothers' house on the market, too.

Things were going along snag-free, and for a while, I was actually starting to breathe. No, not *easier*—after months of feeling like I was holding my breath, I felt like I was finally just breathing again. And then I started noticing something--Grandma, was starting to experience some dementia. From my work, and the speaking I'd been doing on the subject, I knew she would get worse, never better, and from knowing Grandma, I also knew she would never move from our house into any kind of Senior Care facility, willingly. And so I decided this would be my opportunity to not only honor her-- her fierce privacy, her great beauty, her love of family, but to also practice what I preach: create a memory care environment that I would be pleased to have my family live in. Saying it that way doesn't grasp the large and loving sense of responsibility I felt about creating this design. An anonymous old person wasn't going to be living there, my amazing grandma would be! Although I took it to heart to do my best for others, this was deeply personal.

I got right to work on the renovation using designs for memory challenged seniors that had been tested, and proved effective, in facilities my firm had designed. I also incorporated some design concepts that were new and untested, which I thought would be great. Every detail was considered, in a commercial code way, *and* in a common sense, affordable way, too. At their core, all the design ideas were done to help my grandmother (and parents) live life independently and with dignity for as long as possible. I was so excited to do this for her, my husband worked tirelessly to transform the house to meet their needs.

Perhaps you know the expression that no one is a prophet in their own hometown (or something to that effect?) Well, that was true here, and you can include "or their own family," too. In my field of senior living, I'm considered an "expert." Plus, I've been practicing interior design for over 25 years (with my primary focus of senior living design for 20.) Yet, it became clear that there was no prophet to be found anywhere near, or around, South Parkview Avenue, in Columbus, OH.

The issue came into focus early on. In these intertwined lives of my life, my Parents and some of my siblings believed I was designing the spaces incorrectly, which (to them) meant that living in the house could, or even *would,* cause harm to my grandmother, or my parents. My challenge was clear: I somehow needed to shift expectations from, *"Let's dumb down spaces for the good of our home's senior population,"* to a more elevated expectation of, *"The more active they are, the better they will be, both mentally and physically."* The design phase was easy compared to the shifting belief phase that followed it.

As anyone who has any type of arthritis knows, with arthritis moving can be a challenge and when stationary for too long, it's even worse. Like getting a long train moving down the tracks, the wheels grind and require maximum effort to get moving, but once they do, once the rust is all knocked off, and the wheels actually start moving, they turn pretty smoothly, and with very little effort. Today, with our mobility scooters, lift chairs, and walkers, many people have adapted the mindset that when physical difficulties come a callin', you let off the gas, settle for less, and watch yourself continually decline.

Not in this house.

Sorry Mom, sorry Dad, sorry Grandma, but that way of thinking goes completely against what I was taught at my first senior living design job at Karrington Assisted Living (now Sunrise) where I was Director of Interior Design. Here's what you could expect at Karrington: if you rolled in in a wheelchair, we'd have you in a walker in two weeks; if you ambulated in using a walker, a cane was waiting for you in two weeks, and if you hobbled in using a cane, two weeks later we'd be sure the handrail was your new best friend/ support system. Karrington understood that muscles decline, and two weeks was the magic number it took to build them back up again. More than that, though, they also understood they'd not only be building up the body, but the mind and spirit, also. I saw this happen time and time again. And so we encouraged residents to use the stairs. Yes, you read that right, and we told them it wasn't how fast they did them, but simply that they did them. When there were challenges around mobility, our therapists got folks up and about and eventually moving to the stairs. When medicine is regulated, and bifocals are properly adjusted, stairs can be the best form of exercise a senior can utilize.

So why am I telling you all this? My design for our home was focused on getting that long train back running on two sets of tracks. One set pointed in the direction of my grandma's Bedroom Suite, and the other set went up the stairs to my Parents' 2nd floor suite. And in 2014, with all of these controversial renovations completed, our family moved in together. The move was most difficult for my grandmother, as would be expected, when change takes place for someone with Alzheimer's/Dementia. Yet, with all the snags and plot twists, we did it!

And so we embarked on what I call our "4-Gen Social Experiment," which was such a more fun and hip way to think of it as opposed to calling it, "*Living with my Parents, Grandma, Husband, two Kids, and a dog.*" We were all here, living with the many, many tangible "design items" I'd thought about when drawing up our plans. I knew the home needed to be inter-generational, and knew that its outside needed to draw us into its beauty. I understood the home would need to have spaces where everyone could have privacy, could escape, and would never feel as though they were a burden. Finally, though, I realized what would be the most important ingredient of all—and it was an intangible one: *appreciation*. Appreciation that the environment would not be perfect, no matter how hard we tried and no matter how many details were considered. Appreciation of the fact that this would be hard on everyone and that flexibility would be required. Appreciation in understanding that as life changes the environment would also have to. And finally appreciation in knowing that, at whatever age, we would all be getting the gift of "*doing life.*" Whether we were 16, 19, 46, 47, 72, 74 or 92, we were all getting to do this social experiment together, we were all figuring out what works and doesn't together, and hopefully, we were all, along the way, having a richer and fuller life experience, together.

It's said that the quality of one's life is more important than the longevity of one's life; my company's mission is to improve quality of life by design. My family has always lived full, rich lives, adding value to each other's lives as we've loved one another, and followed our dreams.

And so we move forward… four generations under one roof, in Columbus, Ohio, where "my little social experiment," is really the physical fulfillment of the bond that ties us together, and where I'm just carrying on the long tradition of giving back to my family. And it's all normal to me.

CHAPTER 2

THE HIVE

We are beekeepers here in the 4-Generation experiment. Literally, since late spring of 2016, my husband announced that we were now the proud owners of a beehive. It was an announcement that took me by surprise, but his reasons made a lot of sense: it would give Grandma another nice activity, one that didn't require a big outlay of energy from her, (she *is* 94 years old!), it would also give my mother a nice way to take a break in her busy day, a lot of which involves caretaking Grandma, and of course, we'd all reap the rewards of the fresh honey. And so we became involved in the daily goings-on of our family's beehive.

I wasn't an expert before, and I'm not much of one now, but the more I watch these bees, the more I'm convinced that we, and they, have an awful lot more in common than our passion for honey. One day, while I was watching the bustle of the bees, I had a strange thought--what if someone was watching *our* house, in the same way I was sitting here watching *their house*, their beehive? What if someone was at their window observing our comings and goings like I was observing theirs? What would they see? I realized right then that they'd see some very startling similarities between us.

The hive for us is our house. And here, in our multi-generational experiment, we're living all together in a confined space; and the bees are doing the same. In the wintertime, just like our bees, we too become shut-ins. And just like in a beehive, here in Bexley, Ohio, if you don't define your roles, your boundaries, don't know where people go, or understand how they live together, it's not a successful way to live. To put it another way, the hive won't thrive. Anyone watching our "hive/home would see that we, like our bees, do very bee-like things: we take care of each other, we sacrifice for each other, we defend our hive.

They'd see people in their cars coming in and out all day long, and just from watching us, they'd be able to identify which roles we all play in our hive. Greg and I are the "worker bees" going out to support the hive; we do it by making money the same way bees in the hive do it by making honey. We have "nurse bees" that are caretakers, like my mom, and even, Jake and Addie, when they're home. We have our "guard bees" that defend, and protect, sitting on the porch of our house/hive; here we call them, Dad or Grandpa, and Callie our dog. And of course, they'd occasionally spot our "Queen" herself, who all of this is done in service to. Our Queen Bee is Grandma. Everything is set up for her benefit, and everyone else works around her, accompanying her needs. She's protected, watched over, and only goes out at certain times (every Thursday and some Fridays.) This is exactly what happens in the beehive with their Queen. (By the way, my mom's a part-time Queen.)

Having this beehive image in my mind provided me with a little bit of relief. I recognized that I didn't have to be everything and do everything, and that my mom doesn't, either. It's not all on any one of us-- it's all of us together, doing what's best for our hive. There's comfort knowing that each one of us has certain duties and responsibilities, and even more comfort knowing that if we fulfill them, we'll all be okay.

This idea of being a responsible member of a team is what I think it used to mean to "be a family." It's what they did: took care of each other, respected each other's needs, sacrificed for the greater good, supported each other in tough times, as well as good ones, and stayed connected with each other. The benefits of those actions come into sharp focus when you're living with multiple generations. When young kids watch Bing Crosby movies with the older folks (or engage with them in many other ways), they become less siloed into their own generational world. In the process, they become more tolerant of and empathic towards others whose lives are very different than theirs. They are constantly being exposed to their elders' wisdom and calm slow ways. The flip side of it is, the older ones are grabbing onto the young ones, and extracting their energy, spirit and optimism. And for Greg and me? We are getting the chance to connect on a much deeper level with both sides because of our shared "hive." We hear conversations going on and we're much richer for them. It causes us to have conversations with all of them, too. For me, living with my parents and grandmother lets me hear stories that I'd never have had the chance to hear before, and might not have the chance to ever, but living together in the hive there are wonderful, funny, sad, poignant stories that come out in the natural course of our daily lives. When the elders pass, their stories will live on, and in that way, so will they.

CHAPTER 3

PARKVIEW

Before we embark on our journey of discovering "How to Stay Alive in the Hive," I want to orient you to the layout of the house, showing you both the before and the after of the renovation we did here. My hope is that using this will help you better understand how the spaces were manipulated, and where our "Field Notes" actually take place.

In drawing the floorplans, I realized that when it came to our renovation work, we touched very little square footage. This was a delightful surprise to me; it let me see, very tangibly, something I believe wholeheartedly...that small modifications often create exponential, positive impact for the entire family.

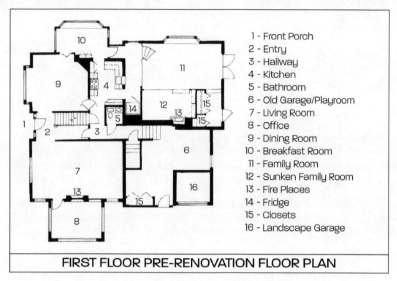

1 - Front Porch	
2 - Entry	
3 - Hallway	
4 - Kitchen	
5 - Bathroom	
6 - Old Garage/Playroom	
7 - Living Room	
8 - Office	
9 - Dining Room	
10 - Breakfast Room	
11 - Family Room	
12 - Sunken Family Room	
13 - Fire Places	
14 - Fridge	
15 - Closets	
16 - Landscape Garage	

FIRST FLOOR PRE-RENOVATION FLOOR PLAN

Diagram A: 1st Floor *Pre-renovation* Plan of Our House

You enter the house from the front porch and immediately see the stairs to the second floor. Straight back from the entrance and to the right of the stairs there is a door. Through the door, a hallway leads to the kitchen and a bathroom. If you go down 5 stairs you'll find an enclosed garage that was converted to a playroom prior to our move in. To the right of the entry, you will find the living room, and an office (that we later converted to a bedroom). To the left is the dining room, and further left, you'll find the breakfast room. Off the dining room and breakfast room is the kitchen. And if you go past the kitchen, you'll be in the family room, complete with its sunken portion and fireplace (both dating back to an addition in the 1970's, which was probably obvious!)

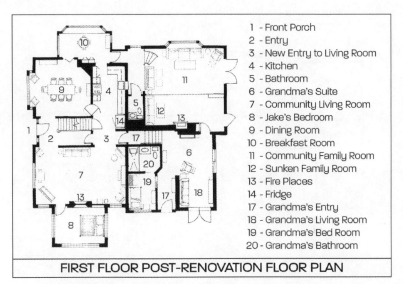

1 - Front Porch
2 - Entry
3 - New Entry to Living Room
4 - Kitchen
5 - Bathroom
6 - Grandma's Suite
7 - Community Living Room
8 - Jake's Bedroom
9 - Dining Room
10 - Breakfast Room
11 - Community Family Room
12 - Sunken Family Room
13 - Fire Places
14 - Fridge
17 - Grandma's Entry
18 - Grandma's Living Room
19 - Grandma's Bed Room
20 - Grandma's Bathroom

FIRST FLOOR POST-RENOVATION FLOOR PLAN

Diagram B: 1ˢᵗ Floor *Renovated* Floor Plan of Our House

Upon the completion of the renovation, we achieved exactly what we'd hoped to…we'd liberated the first floor from its constricted, siloed spaces, and restored the flow. The primary elements of the renovation on the 1ˢᵗ floor included the rearrangement of the kitchen and bathroom; by opening up a wall in the living room we allowed you not to get trapped in the space once you entered. Now, you could enter off the entry, and exit by the kitchen *or* to Grandma's Suite. We took the enclosed garage/play room and converted it to Grandma's Suite, with its bedroom, bathroom, living room and entry. A door was created off her suite to the community family room. Then we opened up the family room by removing the bookcases and a closet; this created views that weren't restricted and a space that wasn't constricted. Finally, by moving the bathroom from the hallway, the kitchen became one space, which not only remedied those pinched spaces, it also opened the room for better circulation.

SECOND FLOOR PRE-RENOVATION FLOOR PLAN

Diagram C: 2ⁿᵈ Floor Existing Floor Plan of Our House

Ascending the 16 steps to the second floor, you find yourself on a landing. This becomes the central hub that all the entries of our second floor rooms converge around. The second floor includes one master bedroom, one common bathroom, three bedrooms, and one laundry room.

15 - Closets
21 - Landing
22 - Master Bedroom
23 - Common Bathroom
24 - Addie's Bedroom
25 - Bedroom 2
26 - Bedroom 3
27 - Laundry Room
28 - Flat Roof
29 - Master Bath
30 - Shared Laundry

SECOND FLOOR POST-RENOVATION FLOOR PLAN

Diagram D: 2ⁿᵈ Floor Renovated Floor Plan of Our House

Our primary objectives here were: to create a living suite for my parents, while maintaining privacy for all parties (my husband and me, and our daughter are all up here, too), and to keep the laundry on the 2ⁿᵈ floor.

One of the existing bedrooms became my parents' den; the other would become their bedroom. Converting the extremely large laundry room to their bathroom, with a shared laundry, was the most economical decision, as the space was already plumbed. Off the new bathroom, the existing exterior flat roof was converted to a private patio suite, and voila... a living suite was created for my parents with a den, bedroom, private bathroom and private exterior patio. And the shared laundry between the master bedroom hallway and their bathroom proved to be convenient for all.

CHAPTER 4

MY GRANDMA: GERLINE ELIZABETH FINK LILLY

I've been a little peeved at my mom recently. Mad that she never told me that this woman, my grandma, had done so much in her life, so much more than birth two children and make great pies. I'm not saying there's anything wrong with birthing two kids and making pies--I've done one of those and wish I could do the other. But I realize now that all the positives were heaped on my grandfather, a self-educated man who listened to opera and sat on the board of Summers County Historical Society and received a "History Hero" award from the Senate of West Virginia. And my grandmother? She was "a homemaker." Much later, I discovered she was that, and a lot more, too. And I guess that's what makes me perturbed, especially the later part because "later" means now, and "now" means Alzheimer's.

I had no idea she loved sports and played basketball, no idea she played the violin in her high school orchestra, and not a clue that she sang so beautifully that she was cast in the lead in her high school's musicals. The Grandma I knew was prim and proper; her lipstick was always on and she always had lots of cozy blankets that she piled on us in the winter. The Grandma I remember never drove, she combed my grandpa's hair, and packed him a perfect lunchbox every day. Whatever your idea of what an ideal grandma is, that's who mine was.

And now that I think about it, maybe I'm not as irritated at my mother as I am at myself. All these years I only saw Grandma one dimensionally, and now I wish I had gotten to know her in all of her multi-dimensional glory. I wonder what stories she would have remembered that now she can't, what conversations we would have that now we won't; mostly, I wonder what I would have learned from her. All of those chances that are gone forever, and I can't help feeling like I was robbed (and yes, I know that sounds selfish of me.)

What if I had a stronger connection with her earlier on in my life? Well, aside from thinking how much fun it would have been to have heard *her* stories as told *by her*, (because no one else can really ever tell our stories like we can), I would have liked to have had her as a role model. Had I known that Grandma was a leader, a sports person, a person who thought a lot about life things, I think our connection could have been so much deeper, and I know her thoughts could have guided me. Today, the connection we have is different. Conversations go in and out; sometimes she doesn't know we've even had a conversation.

It's so powerful to have elders around, guiding you throughout the big and little times of your life. It's a missing component for me, and I think it's true in our society, too. It's so different knowing a person as someone with Alzheimer's/Dementia than if you knew them before that. We give them a different level of respect, and don't see their Alzheimer's/Dementia as their only dimension. Imagine if you did not know that Glen Campbell was a famous singer or that Ronald Regan was a movie star and President of the United States. How differently would you respond to them without this knowledge of what they had accomplished prior to having Alzheimer's/Dementia?

Today, I'm trying to look at the good that's overshadowing my disappointment and sadness. A lot of it comes from living within our 4-Generation Social Experiment. One thing I've realized is that there's something great about being a witness to the whole life cycle. It's hard, but also amazing to see it and to be around those different souls who are in their different seasons. It's an education every day to watch them handle things based on all the life experiences they've had. I think it balances all of us who are living under this roof. Life here is like a complex, well-balanced dish that has so many flavors. Each bite is rich and so delicious--each taste makes you say, *"Ahhhh."* Taken apart and eaten on their own, those same flavors are just not as great--one's too bland, one's too spicy, another is too sweet, another too salty. It's easy to forget how much these "souls" season our life's dishes, how they make them delicious in ways we never expected. Those souls are what make me look around our home all the time and say, *"This really is so good!"* Without Grandma, and the complexity of who she is today, as part of our mix around here, ours would just be life without seasoning.

And so for me, as I look at all the positives, I've realized that I have an obligation with my own kids, my nieces, nephews, and, at some point, my grandchildren. I always want to talk openly and honestly about my earlier life, what I did, what I cared about, who I really was: the good, the bad, and the unsavory. Today, I'm choosing to have conversations as a mother, aunt and also as a mentor and a guide. So if you're in my home, you can be pretty sure about three things: I'll give you great pie (that I *didn't* make), I'll give you a cozy blanket to snuggle under, and I'll engage with you, maybe I'll ask some tough questions. Because I know this for sure, I don't want to have regrets when I'm old for not knowing you, and I don't want you to have regrets for not knowing me, the way I do for not knowing Grandma in the way I'd like to today.

In writing this, I texted my mother and asked her if she had Grandma's High School yearbook. She asked Grandma and her reply was, *"I know I have a High School annual…my Mom would know where it is."* The moral of the story is to engage and ask while you can still get an answer.

CHAPTER 5

GRANDMA'S APARTMENT SUITE

Prior to my parents moving in, I came home from work expecting the usual: kids' stuff everywhere, dog hoping to go out etc. Imagine my surprise when, with my very first step into the house, I caught my parents engaged in a completely different activity...counting the stairs! Imagine their guilt when they found themselves caught! When I asked, "What are you doing?" They were very clear in their response, "We're counting! There are twice as many steps here than where we are living now." "NO. It's exactly the same as you have," I told them, "And, by the way, if you were in physical therapy you'd just go up and down, without challenging." It deteriorated from there. Clearly, the social experiment was having one of its "hiccups" and it had not even technically started! Actually, it was having the first of two hiccups over this issue, because on yet another day, I caught them again, this time measuring the stairs!

Let me get right to the point of this chapter: Grandma moves up and down the steps perfectly. Slower than we do, but she does fine, and she does it with no complaints, and she does it at 94 years of age. It helps her keep fit and keeps her moving in her daily life. Even though her memory has gotten worse, her physical stamina has gone up since she's moved in with us; she's so much more active, and her life is so much more about moving from inside to outside. And it's the same for my parents, despite all their new math calculations and applications in the home.

Now let me go back to what all preceded this.

My parents were looking to move to a ranch house. They'd both had knee surgeries, and my mother also had back and shoulder surgeries; Grandma, who lived with them, was showing more and more signs of Alzheimer's/Dementia. The ranch house felt like a safe and healthy option. Today we live in a two-story, old Dutch Colonial. The home is on a sloped site that, with the multiple additions through the years, has created lower levels that don't make it a three-story but make the first floor have 5 steps from the rest of the house to Grandma's apartment or the family room. We also have a full basement, which we need for everyone's stuff (1 Great Grandmother, 2 Grandparents, 2 Parents and 2 Teenagers + Callie the rescue dog) almost on a daily basis.

Right off the bat, my design called for my parents to move up to the second floor of our house. The design also had five steps that grandma had to walk down to get to her apartment suite, and yes, the same five steps would be required for her to get up into the kitchen and dining room to socialize with the rest of us in the house.

The results of my design decision were amazing! Just like clockwork, my parents complained! And then… they started to move! Like slugs! Up and down the steps for the first two weeks. Remember the people at Karrington (now Sunrise), the company I learned senior living and Alzheimer's/Dementia design from, turns out they knew what they were talking about regarding muscles needing two weeks to shape up!

And as for my grandmother, she did not complain. But she went slowly, really slowly, until imagine what happened next—at that magical two-week marker: her muscles also started to form, and she started to move more easily.

And so, after a couple of weeks, no one was complaining, no one was worrying (well, about that, we *are* a big Italian family and so there's always worrying about something...that's for another book.) And everyone even had more energy. I'll go into a deeper discussion about how to make things easier in the pages to come, but for now, don't confuse making something "easier," with reducing what someone is capable of doing. Easier in this book means removing obstructions that get in the way of someone being their best, and while the stairs started out definitely the opposite of "easier," over time they were exactly what was needed for everyone to step up (literally) into their greatest selves.

Designing Grandma's Apartment

When it came time for me to sit down and design Grandma's apartment, I hit on an easy to remember design philosophy, which is remarkably similar to a life philosophy: "LOVE." Light, Optimize, Visual & Ease.

If you design with "LOVE", you increase independence and dignity. Designing with LOVE means you're allowing the person suffering from Alzheimer's/ Dementia to be their best them at that moment in time. And designing with LOVE gives you the flexibility to adapt to their ever-changing needs. That all sounds so positive and enlightened, but oddly enough, the LOVE Method caused a very non-loving response between all of our family. The LOVE Method caused me to argue with my siblings and parents about how to best design the environment for my grandmother. Today, two years since the renovation took place, and a little over a year of living in this social experiment began, I can say that the LOVE Method works.

Some of what I implemented for Grandma was different than what I would do in an assisted living home. Here, in my own home, I was able to experiment with what I felt would work best vs. what code requires when designing a commercial space for seniors. And

Grandma's bedroom is one such place, where the minimum square footage requirements in senior living are much larger than the space I had to work with here.

What helped me wrap my head around the design was something I noticed about myself. I travel three to four days a week, and I noticed something about myself: I often can't remember the layout of the hotel room when I am trying to find the bathroom in the middle of the night. I get up, am disoriented and sometimes I am the thing that goes "bump in the night." And yes, in more extreme cases, I'm the thing that goes bump and falls in the night. Though I don't have Alzheimer's/Dementia, I do have difficulty when in a new environment and just waking up. So I reasoned that my grandmother who may not remember her bedroom layout may be just as disoriented as I get in various hotel rooms, perhaps even more. In nursing homes, it is common when someone is a fall risk to place their twin bed up against a wall. This would help them to not get trapped on the inside wall if they rolled out of bed. It also helped to create muscle memory, so we tried the same concept of only allowing her one option to enter and exit her bed. The intention of the design was to create EASE for my grandmother, reducing choices and creating muscle memory.

Grandma's suite was designed to have a living room, bedroom, bathroom and outdoor entry. We added large French and sliding doors to any outside wall possible, (if there was a wall that was not connected to the inside of the house – meaning if it could have a window or door placed in it to the outside to bring in natural light, then we put them in. We were employing the first letter of the Love design philosophy = Light. We put integral blinds into the French doors so that she would not get them all gibber jawed by playing with them. Integral blinds mean that the mini blinds are sandwiched in between the panes of glass. They can still be opened, closed raised up or down at any height. They are safe and do need to be cleaned. We also placed a window in her bedroom. Since the brain's alarm clock is kicked off by light, which produces melatonin, the benefit of all this natural light was to help Grandma sleep normal vs. waking up in the night. Natural light would also help cue her to the time of day. This would be a big help to early stage Alzheimer/Dementia folks like Grandma, helping her to recognize the difference between breakfast and dinner and the appropriate time to go to bed.

The third letter in the LOVE design philosophy is Visual. The key idea here was separating the spaces as much as possible. I wanted Grandma to understand the reasons for the spaces, for their design to be apparent. Doing this would help her be less confused by her environment, or so I hoped. When she walked into her apartment, I wanted it to be easy for her to understand the purpose of each space, and to know what to expect. If she did, it would help her be less agitated, again, "or so I hoped." Her easily understood spaces would allow Grandma to have a higher level of independence; she'd be able to enjoy moving from one area to another for specific reasons that would engage her, and the way they were designed reinforced their purpose. The key thought behind designing for a senior with memory issues is this: when dealing with people who are already confused, don't confuse them further by the interior design. Taking this to heart meant, for me, having Grandma's apartment work with her, not against her.

If you can't quite understand how difficult it is for someone with Alzheimer's/Dementia on a daily basis, I would ask that you do these three exercises and then write down how you felt. Understanding where they are helps you meet them where they are and reduce stress for everyone. Emotional understanding is just as, if not more, important than a physically supportive space. When you have both, it's a winning combination for everyone.

Exercise 1:

Take a piece of paper and write your name and birth date with your ***non-dominant*** hand. Now write how this made you feel.

Everyday a person with Alzheimer's/Dementia feels this way. They know they were better, yet somehow now slower and disconnected, frustrated, and sometimes it's difficult to even get your brain around how to form the letters. It takes extreme effort and concentration, and yet you've been doing this for years! Imagine 80 years…. You know your name and when you were born, but trying to get it on paper legibly and fast is a task. The brain takes up to 25% of the oxygen needed in your body, which is why mental work is so exhausting.

Exercise 2:

Take out a piece of paper and write down all you did in 30 minute increments 2 days ago……from the time you got up till when you went to sleep. Most people don't get very far. Write down how this makes you feel. Now remember how we snicker when grandma can't remember if she took her pills today or ate breakfast. The more someone sleeps, the more difficult remembering becomes.

Exercise 3:

Place your index finger pointed at the sky above your nose (with your head looking up) now turn your finger slowly clockwise, while slowly moving it down (yet close to your body) till it's at your nose and then lower it continuing to turn it clockwise….. now your head should be looking down at your finger and what do you notice? If you have done the exercise correctly your finger has switch to counterclockwise. Magic? Confused? I bet you are; most people will do this 2-3 times before they believe it.

Write down how this made you feel.

What happened? Your perspective changed. My grandmother experiences the world different than I do because her perspective is different due to the dementia. All the explaining to her in the world can't make her understand my finger was going clockwise if she's looking down on the finger and I am looking up on the finger.

What if every day or hour or minute your perspective changed and disoriented you to understanding your reality? Seems pretty cruel, and then you have people that you thought you were safe with and that loved you arguing with you and you know your right but they tell you you're not. So you become a bit untrusting and paranoid, they are crazy, not you, right? This happens with my grandma taking her pills, she believes that she has taken them and her perspective says she's 100% right so why would someone force her to take more unless they were trying to hurt her.

This simple exercise can help caregivers, spouses, and family members to understand the change in perspective of someone like my grandmother with Alzheimer's/Dementia and adapt to using positive manipulation techniques to help get through the normal functions of life vs. arguing with their loved one.

Exercise 4:

This exercise comes from Z-Health. You will need 2 people for this exercise and a cell phone to video.

Blindfold yourself and have the other person video you. If possible, place ear buds or ear protection in your ears to help reduce sound. Now march in place for a minute.

Take off the blindfold and take out the ear buds (if you had them) and see where you are standing now...

What happened? When we take away our sight and lose some of our hearing, it is often more difficult than one would expect to understand where we are in this world and that we are moving, even when we think we are staying in one place.

Recognize that aging adults have lost a substantial amount of their senses, from sight to hearing, touch and on.

The largest lesson from these exercises is to have empathy so that we can meet them where they are. When we come from a place of understanding others and their challenges, communication and connection are increased, which is in direct correlation to having a wonderful quality of life.

CHAPTER 6

GRANDMA'S LIVING ROOM

From her apartment's living room, Grandma looks out onto a beautiful magnolia tree. It's the same tree my husband, Greg, and I see from our bedroom (since our room's back deck is attached to hers), and the same one my parents see from their bathroom and private deck. One day, not too far into the "experiment," we noticed Grandma outside by herself wandering around. Had we been asleep, or in the middle of winter, this could have been tragic. We got her inside and it was as though she was channeling the great Houdini himself: she escaped again. Even though we had locked all the doors. This happened several times and soon we had to make a decision: we would have to take away some of her independence in order for her to be safe. Greg went out and got new locks for her apartment that would be difficult to open for her. Honestly, I don't think Grandma was trying to escape, but I also honestly don't think she realized the dangers out there: we have a pool and we also have brick steps, a fall into or on either of those would be a disaster. It's tricky because Grandma is a "living" person who's living her life —and that's great, except when it isn't, because it's scary, dangerous, frustrating, and more.

The idea of what it means to be "living" when someone has Alzheimer's/Dementia is something I think about all the time. So,

I guess it was natural that when it came time to design her actual Living Room, there was a lot I wanted for Grandma, and a lot of ideas were burning in my brain.

I wanted a separate room for her, one that would get her out of and off her bed to socialize, rather than lying on her bed and sleeping for large parts of her day. It's interesting, when we're younger and full of life, when we're just doing life so hard, we have to work to find time to sleep. But when we get old, when we're slowing down so much, we have to work to find ways to do more life and less sleep. Less sleep means more engaging. Sleeping less also means feeling less groggy, and spending less time in that woozy state between sleep and awake, a state that, when Grandma's in it, she often seems more confused than she actually may be.

And so, to avoid having her spend so much time in that "pre-coffin" of hers: aka her bed, I designed a separate living space or living room. Here, she can entertain us, her friends, and even the dog. Her living room lets her socialize more; it forces her to go out and interact; it pulls her into engagement, into laughter, and gives her more opportunities to be touched. Her Living Room really helps keep her living life.

Another critical design element that informed my plan for Grandma's living room was light. In the LOVE design philosophy, which I already mentioned, L stands for "Light," and I wanted there to be lots of it, for as many day time hours as possible, helping cue her body's internal clock as much as it could. The sliding French doors we added to her outside walls helped us bring in all the light we could. The integral blinds they have built inside of them, keep things simple and impossible for Grandma to tinker with, providing her with light and safety and security.

Some extra security measures were needed here, too, because as I said above: Grandma kept getting out. And though we told her not to unlock the doors, she kept ignoring us. (Actually, it was unclear if she was ignoring, being obstinate or had just forgotten the conversation.) One thing about senior living that I've noticed is their tactile fascination; sometimes they're like kids playing with switches, locks, etc., and Grandma is no different than her peers in this area, especially with locks - she can jimmy her way out of the best of them! We thought the deadbolt and other locks would work, but with all her tinkering she figured them out, and so we put an extra lock system into it, and also added "sliders" bolstered with security locks on them. It's worked…for now. But the other thing about Alzheimer's/Dementia design is that there's a need to be ever vigilant and notice what changes have happened, or are in the process of happening, and then react to them prior to an issue.

In Grandma's living room, she has a "sit-to-stand" recliner, an end table, and a sofa, for guests and a TV. As most seniors do, she watches quite a bit of TV, and she has her favorites: sports being one. Back in High School, Grandma played guard on her basketball team, so we'll often find her engaged in a game that's on TV. She was also the lead in her High School play (yes, apparently, Grandma was one of the "popular" kids) and today you can find her watching any TV show where music is involved: The Voice, America's Got Talent, American Idol…she loves watching them all; they lift her spirits. The nice thing about this is that the way her living room is set up, others can watch with her, too. This is something I considered when designing the layout. We don't have to sit there for a visit and stare at each other; the space is designed to alleviate that awkwardness. I think that too often we can confuse actually needing to engage, with just sitting and being with her. I sometimes go in, sit on the couch and watch TV with her, not so much to talk to her, but just to sit and keep her company. Sharing the space is comforting…for both of us. It's a way to connect, to re-connect and to stay connected.

The recliner was something we thought she'd use differently than she does use it. We expected to see her using it to get up and down out of the chair, but as is so often the case, what we thought and what's Grandma's reality are two different things. She uses the recliner to sit in it to watch TV, and then she leans back and naps. Regardless, of how she uses it, it's a great addition to the space.

Mentally, she's always trying to push herself, and wanting to make things easier. She doesn't want to be a burden, so in her mind, as long as she can get in and out of that chair, she knows she can also get in and out of other chairs, too--in our breakfast room, our dining room, and living room. And so that chair has become a little bit like her own personal, in house (literally!) Physical Therapist.

The recliner, which is plugged in to an electric outlet, has been a source of unintentional drama and humor, too. We have a "Piper," a system worth considering if you're planning on conducting your own multi-generational "experiment" at home. It's a little camera, and all you do is go to an app, turn it on and you can see if your loved one is doing okay, or needs assistance. For us, it's allowed my mom more peace of mind, and now we also keep it on all night. Plus, Grandma was getting out the front door when she wasn't supposed to, so this helps us keep better track of her whereabouts, while still giving her some freedom from our watchful eyes. The problem we didn't expect was a power outage, two of them, actually. One occurred when my parents were out, and they called us to check on her because the Piper was not coming on. When my daughter got home and went into Grandma's apartment to check on her, sure enough, Grandma was stuck right where she'd been when the power went out: leaning way back in her recliner... and yes, she couldn't get out. Adellina had to work hard, and for quite a while, to get Grandma out. Drama and humor meet fairly often in our house, and it's a good thing, it makes a lot of situations that are tough, a little easier to bear...for all of us. Grandma was thankful and gracious and Adellina was happy to help.

When it came time to decide what surface to have on the floor, we decided on carpet, wall-to-wall, and for a number of very conscious reasons. One, it was what she was used to in her own home. Here, in her living room, I made sure it was a very dense pile so that she doesn't trip on it if she, like many seniors, starts to have the front part of her foot "drop." When that happens, it starts causing people to trip over their own feet, but a low cut, dense pile that doesn't part when Grandma pulls up her foot, lets us lessen the potential of her falling. But if she were to have an accident and fall, a softer surface gives us hope that maybe she won't break anything. And then there's another reason for this kind of dense pile, and that has to do with the other kind of "accident." If Grandma doesn't make it to the bathroom, a sad reality for a senior of her age, it's much easier to clean up this kind of carpet.

A final reason for the carpet decision is its ability to help to absorb the noise. A hard surface makes the noise bounce. When that happens, Grandma needs to turn the TV up higher, and higher. (And it's usually up pretty high to start with.) Also, if she's agitated, or irritated, or in pain, we notice that noise agitates her more, so Grandma's softer, smoother environment really helps to reduce her agitation.

And now a word about light sensors: they're great, definitely use them when you need them. As I've talked about before, Grandma has five stairs off her Living Room, so to keep her safe we put a light sensor on them. It goes on automatically when it senses her movement, which is great because we don't have to worry about her remembering to turn on the light when she's moving around. We also have a railing on one side of the steps and wanted to be sure she used it, which meant being sure she *saw* it. (It's not rocket science, folks, most times it's just common sense.) So rather than it being the same color as the wall and blending into the wall, we stained it so that it would contrast with the wall color. This makes the railing "pop," and as of this writing, she hasn't missed seeing it yet!

At the top of those stairs we made another purposeful design decision: we moved the door out to give her a three-foot landing. Now, when she's getting ready to open the door to go to the rest of the house, we don't worry about her teetering on the top step before going in, or out. She gets to her landing, pauses, gets her footing, gets her balance and then moves to where she needs to be. It's just a simple landing before opening the door, but it makes a huge difference for her. In fact, just these few little things for her stairs:

light, handrail contrast, the landing...makes the steps so much easier for her to use. If we had made it difficult for her to use, she wouldn't come into the rest of the house as much, and that's the opposite of what we wanted for her. This is a great example of the E = Ease in the Love Design Philosophy. We wanted her to be all around the house, engaging with us, not cooped up in her apartment all day. And so far, to a pretty great extent, we've succeeded.

Chapter 7

Grandma's Bedroom

Typically, most people would have looked at the space we had for Grandma's apartment and made the living room and bedroom one space. I took the space and divided it to create her living space, vestibule, and her connected bedroom and bathroom. This "divide" would help cue her to the space's intended activity.

The "bedroom" is a private space; it's for sleeping and getting dressed and undressed, only. In it you won't find a chair or sofa, because this would be confusing to her. What's there is a twin bed, and it's there for sleeping. The "living space" is for exactly that - *living* or socializing, it's the place of her awake time. To eat, she would need to leave her suite, navigate those five stairs to get to the kitchen and dining room.

This design was all about one thing: reducing everything to its absolute single purpose. So it was fine that the bedroom was smaller, fine that it could only fit a twin bed, and fine that that bed is pushed against the wall to her left. This made the next choice clear: place her nightstand and dresser to her right. Now Grandma has only one choice: get out of bed to the right. And before bed or a nap, she has only one choice, too: put her glass of water on the table to her right. This employs the "O" in the "LOVE" Design Philosophy, which stands for: *Optimize*.

The idea behind my design is simple: if I'm decreasing the choices she has to make, I'm increasing her chances of her making the right ones. It's like getting on a highway and you come upon signs going all different directions where multiple highways converge. The choices are too many and poor you, you don't have a GPS to guide you *and* you've never been there before. It's suddenly gotten a lot harder to make the right choice and a lot more nerve racking. But if you're on the road and there's only one off-ramp, it's hard to make the wrong choice, your stress is reduced and you have a much larger chance that you made the right choice.

There's another reason for limiting Grandma's choices. Let's look at her bed again. There it is against the wall. There Grandma is, *not* making a choice in how she's going to get up, she's just going one way. So not only does this help her get up without a hassle, it's also helping her start building muscle memory, which she *can* build vs. mental memory, which she *can't* build anymore and is losing daily. No matter what our age, our body can build muscle memory, and it happens simply by doing the same thing every day in a way that becomes almost automatic. Ever sit down on a toilet at restaurant or airport and felt yourself drop? It's because your derriere is trained to a certain height, most likely the height of the toilet in your home, and you've built muscle memory that tells you how high and where to sit. I'm always looking to improve Grandma's muscle memory, and making her daily choices repetitive and automatic ones, helps accomplish that. Building muscle memory for getting in and out of bed is a great example of the "E" in the "LOVE" Design Philosophy, which stands for: Ease.

One thing I didn't design into her bedroom is a closet. In part it was due to space, but there was something else at work here, too. Everyday my mother lays out Grandma's clothes for her on her bed. This is another way of providing ease in her decisions, and another way of helping her to be more independent, dressing herself is a big part of Grandma's independence, and since we hope that can happen for a long time, we'll do things like this to help encourage it to happen.

Today, Grandma gets up to less confusion, which reduces some of her stress around decision-making. It's stress that comes from her wading through her life and wondering, "*what do I do here, I don't understand.*" Without a lot of decisions required of her, she's able to be more independent, and less frustrated, less anxious and less agitated.

Grandma's bedroom has been familiar to her since way back to move in day, a day that was hard for all of us, but especially hard for her, with her strong reliance on visual cueing and familiarity. The thing we did here to help her was bring her own bed and furniture; it helped her then and continues to do so to this day. She knows her items, her bed, her nightstand, her bedspread. They not only help her to remember, but also help provide her with the great comfort that familiarity brings. We all know that people have relationships to blankets and pillows. This starts early on in our childhood and never seems to leave us. You might be tempted to freshen up with a new look for your loved ones bedding, but I would advise against this. Keep as much as possibly familiar (even if it's a decorator's nightmare). Trust me, if I can do it, you can too.

So though we didn't add bells and whistles, partly because we wanted the space to be able to grow with her as her needs changed, we were also on a budget. What we feel we *did* do was create a manageable "home" within our home for Grandma to live with as much independence and ease as possible.

<u>Bedroom:</u> Physical Do's and Don'ts

Do's:

- Make sure the spaces have as few choices as possible so that muscle memory will take over.
  - o Example – The lamp by the nightstand should only turn on or off by the switch on the lamp. It should not be plugged into an outlet that is tied to a wall switch and therefore be turned off on the wall. Why? Because without a doubt the senior will forget and think the lamp is broken, and when that happens, they'll get frustrated and agitated, possibly get out of bed in the dark and that could lead to a series of new problems/accidents.
  - o If they are by themselves, place the bed against a wall so that they only get out on one side all the time. This will help to avoid confusion and disorientation, especially when waking up in the middle of the night.
- Reduce clutter
- Avoid sharp edges
- Use the senior's furniture and bedding so it is familiar and comforting to them
- Have natural light
- Have large door openings – pocket doors work well for this.
- Have a nightlight (amber color) in the bathroom to help to find at night.

Don'ts

- Don't allow clutter on the floor. Magazines, boxes etc., these are tripping hazards
- Don't have a rug on top of carpet. This can cause a tripping hazard.

- Don't have a footboard on the bed. This can cause the room to feel smaller – make it difficult to make the bed and when hit, cause a bruise or skin tear.
- Don't have extension cords or cords that can be tripped over.
- Don't have a wide open closet. Make their clothing decisions easy by minimizing choices, and only having the clothing in their view they are to put on and wear that day.
- Don't have confusing switches to lights and outlets.
- Don't have lots of seating, unless there is no other space for them to socialize.

CHAPTER 8

GRANDMA'S BATHROOM

My grandmother was the ultimate lady. I had never seen her naked, and for most of my life I'd never even seen her without makeup, her hair done and a nice outfit on. She kept her shape and to this day, at 94 years of age, she is beautiful. She did not grow up in a generation where women went to the "bathroom." They used the "powder room," where they went to powder their nose and apply lipstick—nothing else happened in there. Men were not allowed anywhere near them during this process nor were children. Understanding this helped me to design a space for my Grandma's bathroom that would help her to maintain her dignity and independence for as long as possible, even if she was unaware of her actions.

I was a bit sad when the other day she came out of her room with only her underwear (top and bottom) on asking for help. Out of embarrassment for her, my son laughed nervously. I knew at that moment my grandma was starting to fade into someone that I did not recognize. You see, everyone forgets. Who hasn't lost their keys or can't find their cell phone? But that's not losing a part of yourself, nor is not remembering a name, or if you took your pills. But when she did something so out of character that I knew would mortify her if she was aware of what she was doing, it was like being hit by a ton of bricks.

I feel it's important before we get to know each other further, that I explain to you that these are not just stories to me. They are our life. My hope is that by telling them to you, you might say, *"Oh yeah, that happened to me, too,"* or at least have a heads up to the possibilities of what's coming down the road. These stories translate into real life actionable tips of how to make your family life better through design. Living with someone with Alzheimer's or dementia is like being in a spy movie where your most trusted partner gets brainwashed to forget you and now thinks you're the bad guy. You may have brought him or her back to who they once were, but you're never quite sure which side they are on anymore. I want to believe my grandmother is still in there, and some days, hours or minutes she really is, but without warning she can snap and lose perspective on who we are and our intentions. In these moments, we try to remember that our job is to guide her and reduce the stress of the situation, even if it means agreeing with her reality when we know it's not correct.

Just like in her "bedroom" where the room serves one purpose only, the bathroom follows that same rule. But that came second in my design scheme, first came this simple idea: let's get Grandma into the bathroom *safely,* and that circled back to the idea of having her bedroom and bathroom connected. Today, when Grandma's on her bed, she can see into her bathroom, and one straight path gets her from her bed to the toilet. At night, her nightlight shines a clear path that guides her way; this all helps orient her, and helps her better understand that she was waking up because she had to go to the bathroom.

Connecting her bedroom/bathroom had another thought behind it, too. I was planning for the time when Grandma's ladylike behaviors started diminishing, when my private and proper Grandma would start forgetting about things like closing her bathroom door. With this design, even if the door to her bathroom was open, others wouldn't see her; she wouldn't be exposed, her dignity would be preserved a little longer.

O = Optimize in the Love Design Philosophy. The bathroom space is optimized by *only* having what she needs and nothing that she doesn't. As in her bedroom, this reduces her confusion, stress and frustration. In the bathroom, our lack of space and need to remove obstructions caused us to use pocket doors between her bedroom and bathroom. Having the pocket door to the bathroom open makes it easy to get in and, when open, creates the largest clear floor space for maneuverability and visual cuing. Not only does a "normal" door takes up floor space it's also one more thing for Grandma to manipulate around on the way to, and once inside, the bathroom.

We designed the space to have a shower with seat, a sink and toilet with a bidet seat, it sprays, blow dries, and the seat is heated, some models even have nightlights, something to consider, too. The bidet lets Grandma clean herself, or, if my mother's helping her in this department, it really helps reduce her efforts, and that's a nice plus for her.

It's funny what you think of as "bells or whistles" when you're younger and how they become essentials when you're older, or at least designing for someone who's older. That was the case with something as simple as a heat lamp in the shower. Getting older means losing about 70% of our body fat, and that fat is what's helping us maintain our body temperature, and it's also helping us get "the chill off." Coming out of her shower, Grandma goes from hot to cold with very little insulation. The small addition of a heat lamp in the shower helps warm up the air for her, and lets her step out into a warmer space. For the folks who don't want to take a shower anymore, making the bathroom a warmer, nicer environment is a little thing you can do to make it more enticing.

Also in the bathroom is a combination: light, heat lamp and fan, which doesn't come on automatically. It's located near the shower and she has to turn it on, but usually it's my mother who does this for her, because Grandma is less independent and needs help showering. This is another place where you can take it up to the next step by adding a temperature control setting to make sure the water won't scald anyone. This is great if you're coming in to check on your loved one once a day, or once a week.

Grandma's shower has a curtain, not a glass door. Like most of the decisions I made, this, too, had reasons behind it. A glass door would make it difficult for her to get in and out. Also, since my mom is there helping her shower, the glass door would restrict her movements, making it harder for her to help. And then there was my biggest concern: what if she falls? The glass door could possibly shatter and they could both be hurt. A curtain made a lot more sense.

Even the things that seem like mindless decisions need more thought than you would think: take towels. Standard white, right? Easy and done. Except think again, Grandma's old, her eyes are bad, and without her glasses her world's a blur. Giving her towels that have color provide a contrast to her off-white painted walls. Today she can see her green towels easily without her glasses.

A simple and helpful idea for wall color is to paint the wet wall (the one the toilet is attached to) a brighter color, or accent color. This lets the toilet be clearly visible, and makes it so much easier for someone to see. And for men, it's even more important because they're standing up and aiming. Placing a grab bar behind the toilet at shoulder height allows a man to steady themselves while urinating (in my family we say "peeing"). Putting an amber colored nightlight directly over the top of the toilet, is another thing that helps them aim. In many bathrooms, handrails beside the toilet is a good idea. While we didn't need it because the sink is so close to the toilet that Grandma uses it to steady herself, Greg still added a handrail on the left hand side of the toilet.

Lighting has to be very good in the bathroom, that's obvious, but my decision on "to dim or not to dim" was less obvious. Ultimately, I didn't put the bathroom on a dimmer. I didn't want there to be one more thing for her to have to mess with, and didn't think she needed yet another gadget to cause her confusion: a light switch that isn't quite a light switch? Or, wait, is it? See how easy it could be to get confused? So I opted to use the nightlight to draw her into the bathroom, rather than a dimmer on the main bathroom light. Once inside, she sees a light switch, she hits it and it turns on, she hits it and turns off. It's clear to her. Sometimes the simplest is the best.

Bathrooms are tricky places for the memory impaired, in the same way they were tricky places for small kids. Lots of things in there could be misinterpreted: liquids things that don't look lethal but could be, powdery things that look harmless unless they're consumed, the creams, the ointments, the lotions, the colorful little pills—how do you design for all their needs and still keep them safe yet as independent as possible?

I did it with an easy rule: *"If you don't want them to take it by themselves, don't have it in there."* So, cleaning supplies? Not going to be in there, where Grandma could possibly mistake it for something to drink. Medicine? Not going to be there. Mouthwash? If you drink it, it could be dangerous in excess, but toothpaste is fine. We only have pump soap for her to use for washing; bar soap can get slippery and flip out of her hands, and then she could slip on it.

And then there's her faucet: a one-handled one for Grandma. The pros outweighed any cons. It's a safety thing. With a faucet that has a separate cold and hot lever or knob that you have to turn on each and then blend the water to the right temperature, there's a risk. This goes against the 4th letter of the LOVE design philosophy: "E", which stands for Ease. It's not easy to blend or even to remember the need to do so. The consequences could range from simple discomfort of the water being too cold to scalding herself with the hot water only turned on. With a one-handed faucet there's a much smaller risk of her turning on the wrong one and scalding herself. There *is* one con to take into consideration, if someone has never used a one-handled faucet, they might be confused. You can add to the faucet a temperature controller to ensure that too hot of water does not come out. We have not done this yet but I have it ready to go if need be.

If you're waiting for me to talk about the medicine cabinet in Grandma's bathroom, the wait will be a long one: there isn't one. There's a mirror. But not a medicine cabinet. Every day, my mom comes into Grandma's apartment with a little basket that has Grandma's meds and she gives them to her, eliminating the chance of any medicine cabinet mix-ups, toss-outs, or flush-downs. Things happen as the memory goes. Around here lately, Grandma's become more argumentative and a bit more paranoid. Some days she thinks she already took her meds and that maybe she's being poisoned. In her heart she knows she took them, and she's right, she did…but at another time. Soon we started seeing her hiding them, and soon after that, my mother started becoming more stern with Grandma to take them. Rather than getting into an argument, and saying, *"No, you didn't"* and Grandma would respond, *"Yes I did"* with all the attitude fit for a teenager, whereupon my mother would snap back and off it would go from there, now we just say: *"Yes you did, but this is a new one."* This is part of positive manipulation, getting her to take the medicine; it's telling her a different story.

Finally, the toilet, I actually have a whole chapter detailing this out so be sure to read it for all the details. I may have mentioned that I wanted to test some theories for those with Alzheimer's and Dementia that I have not been able to with my clients. The bidet toilet seat was one of those items. It's a seat that goes onto a conventional toilet and costs about $350.00. You need to have an outlet, which most bathrooms do. The toilet seat makes the seat height correct for a senior, and is antibacterial and antimicrobial. It is warm, can come with a nightlight, and has a sprayer that can be positioned for various private parts, but it only spays if someone is sitting on the seat. It is by far the largest success story of this whole 4-Gen Social Experiment. I was concerned that Grandma would not understand it, I asked her what she thought of it and she said at first she did not know that it was anything special but after my mother showed her what it did she loved it. She felt it was wonderful to be able to give herself a "sitz bath" and reduce the burden on my mother. My mom has let me know on several occasions that if it were to ever break it would be the first thing to be fixed. There may be a time when Grandma can no longer remember to operate it properly but that day is not yet here. When it does come, my mom's effort will be substantially reduced compared to a regular toilet. I believe it is so successful because it engages 3 of the 4 design philosophies in LOVE: Optimize, Visual and Ease.

Looking back at all I've written I realize I probably come across as some kind of a Worst Case Scenario extremist who has a bunker in her backyard filled to the gills with supplies for an inevitable demise of the human race...but that's not me at all. I'm an optimist at heart, and I think that heart can relax, open up and give Grandma so much more love when my brain's not worrying about what might happen next. The key is to make the space easy for her to use, which means the rest of the family does not need to worry with all the "What If" scenarios.

The Bathroom Do's and Don'ts"

Do's

- Have the toilet in view of the bed.
- Have an amber nightlight over the toilet or by the toilet if possible.
- Have a pocket door to the bathroom to allow the entry to be as wide as possible, and ensure at night the door is left open so they can see into the bathroom.
- Have a walk in shower with seat that is easy to use.
- Have a heat lamp. Core body temperatures of seniors are lower so when they get out of the shower it's harder for them to get the "chill" off without the heat lamp.
- Have contrasting color towels so they can be seen easily. A different color than the wall works well.
- Have basic needs such as toothpaste and a tooth brush out and accessible.

- Use the safety latches on cabinets to secure what you want kept safe.
- Provide a trash can in an easy to see and reach space.
- Have a bidet toilet seat for ease of personal cleaning.
- Have a contrasting toilet seat for visual cuing.

Don't

- Don't Have items available that could cause an issue such as cleaning supplies, mouthwash etc.
- Don't have medications accessible that your senior could get into.
- Don't have trip hazards such as rugs.
- Don't have sharp edges, if at all possible.
- Don't have a faucet with 2 blades for water (they may only use the hot or the cold.)
- Don't have carpet as it is difficult to clean if there is an accident, which is more likely closer to the toilet.
- Don't have slippery floors.
- If you have hard floors – avoid tile if possible (vinyl is fine). Grout is difficult to clean and tile is harder if there is a fall, and so it can cause more damage to the body.
- Don't have curling irons, hair dryers etc. accessible.
- Don't have an open drain – change it out so that jewelry, etc. doesn't fall in and get lost.
- Don't use a glass cup for water. Use a plastic or small disposables.

CHAPTER 9

GRANDMA'S CIRCUIT

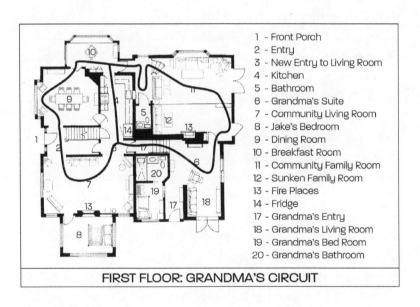

1 - Front Porch
2 - Entry
3 - New Entry to Living Room
4 - Kitchen
5 - Bathroom
6 - Grandma's Suite
7 - Community Living Room
8 - Jake's Bedroom
9 - Dining Room
10 - Breakfast Room
11 - Community Family Room
12 - Sunken Family Room
13 - Fire Places
14 - Fridge
17 - Grandma's Entry
18 - Grandma's Living Room
19 - Grandma's Bed Room
20 - Grandma's Bathroom

FIRST FLOOR: GRANDMA'S CIRCUIT

There's always a certain point when people with Alzheimer's/ Dementia start wandering aimlessly. When we're doing space planning for "Memory Care Neighborhoods" in Assisted Living facilities, one of our goals is *not* having anyone get to the end of a corridor and not know where to go. We're always trying to have them avoid "decision paralysis," which is what happens when they don't know whether to go right or left. If you drove in the pre-GPS

59

era, you might understand what that feels like. Remember a time when you were driving and suddenly weren't sure where you were; you looked around for signs to help you, but there weren't any; you starting feeling a little nervous, anxiety started creeping in, and with no help to decide which way to go, you just stopped. You were paralyzed. That's the same kind of decision paralysis that Alzheimer's/Dementia people deal with *very* frequently.

The good news is, you can lessen their stress enormously. The solution is quite simple, by designing a circular path you are taking away stopping points where they have to make a decision. By letting them keep moving, you are giving them an activity that soothes them instead of frustrates them. You're also allowing them to keep their independence up, by not having to call or ask for help, and their embarrassment down, over not knowing what to do. It's one of those great, and all too rare, things where there are zero negative consequences.

With that in mind, we created a loop, or circuit, for Grandma. We did it even though when she moved from my mom and dad's house to this house she wasn't at the point of wandering around aimlessly, *yet*. But the week she moved in, a death in our family caused her to degrade more quickly than we expected.

Clues started surfacing; she'd say: *"I've got to get my exercise."* She'd never done that before, not just saying that sentence, but the actual *exercising*. It progressed steadily to where she is today: walking aimlessly. That led us to design her loop and now, 99% of the time, she's not frustrated and not paralyzed about where she is or where she should go. She's taking in the sights and sounds of the house, the family and life, and that makes her happy—and us, too.

CHAPTER 10

THE COMMUNITY LIVING ROOM

What does it mean for Grandma to be "living" vs. her being "alive?" How much does she value the emotional parts of life vs. the physical parts of her life? How can we include her in our lives so she never feels that she's a burden, and how can she feel valued? These thoughts were always running through my mind whenever I started designing one of the rooms of our house. And the part about "living" vs. being "alive" was especially strong here, maybe for the obvious reason: it's called the living room, after all.

Grandma's living room is more about her being alive; our community living room is about her *actively living*. It's about her being engaged. Recently, on an early Saturday morning, we were all in there together, when, midstream, Grandma got up and started walking out. When I asked if was she okay, She replied, *"Yes, you're no longer interesting to me."* I guess at 94, when you have a limited amount of time left, you choose your company and conversations carefully. We all loved her answer, and for me, it was doubly great because it meant that our "social experiment" was working: Grandma was still involved, engaged and feisty—she was actively living her life within ours. I think the design of the community living room helps.

Prior to our renovation, the only access to the community living room was from the front entry hall and then… you were stuck. This is not the worst thing in the world if your brain is functioning at its optimum power, but this is not Grandma. She likes to do her "circuits" through the house; she's got a path up, into and all around the house starting from her apartment. These "wandering paths" really help her stay more physically active. But when a room dead-ends, like our community living room did before we remodeled, her wandering path would have turned into a trap, causing her to grow frustrated, disoriented and agitated. So we punched a hole in the wall that was next to the entrance to her apartment and opened it up to the kitchen. Today, this lets her come up right into the community living room, and complete her "circuit." It also lets her be a part of the activity going on in the room.

If you compare and contrast the community living room with Grandma's own living room in her apartment, you'd find it's very similar… just on a larger scale. It turns out the things that were important to Grandma in her living room were also important to us in ours: a lot of sunlight, places to sit and entertain or be entertained. This meant not just a piano, but also a TV.

Having a TV hanging over the fireplace in the community living was a hard pill for me to swallow. Full disclosure: This is not my first "social experiment" in living. My husband, my kids and I had come from living for six months in a no-television experiment that turned into a six-year no-television lifestyle. The point is: we lived without one and actually enjoyed it. I was used to not having the constant influx of daily negativity, and not getting sucked into the endless watching. However, my parents had two mandates: 1.) we had to get cable and 2.) everyone had to be able to watch their own shows, when they wanted to and where they wanted to. This translated into a TV in the community living room. I came around when I asked myself a simple question: *"How can I design things in this house around me when I'm not the one spending 95% of my time there, but they—Grandma, my mom and dad—are?"*

But it wasn't just that, it was also something I learned, that I hadn't ever realized before: the TV is incredibly important to Grandma, and to my parents, too. It's their deep connection to the world. As they go out of the house less, whether due to age, energy levels, ailments or bad weather, they're not just using it for entertainment, but also for news, and sometimes for company. They turn it on in the AM, watch a morning show and get up to speed about what's happening in the world and in our town. I understand now that this is their way of staying in the know, which is a good thing. For Grandma, it's all of those things and one more: it's church—she watches on Sunday.

Because Grandma's a music gal, we decided to place an upright piano in this room, and it makes her really happy to hear it being played. Growing up, Grandma always had music in her life, always loved it, and even played the violin in the High School orchestra. Going down to visit her and my grandfather when I was little, I always remember the two of them together, listening to classical music, which they were brought up on. I also recall that they had the most up-to-date technology to play their music and really enjoy it.

Integrating important pieces from my grandmother's former life was intentional. I wanted her to feel that she was welcome in our community living room. Prominently placing a table that her father made makes Grandma light up every time she sees it, and it draws her into the room. Additionally, her family Bible sits on it, and this is no small Bible. This is a 6 inch high, leather bound, hand-tooled Bible, which she sees and is very proud of.

The other furniture in here: a sofa, a couple of chairs, two small settees and a small card table, is more formal, much fancier, and a little less comfortable than the family room. But regardless of that, Grandma loves this room. She loves its formality, and loves to spend time here. Sometimes she'll come in, sit and look out the windows, some of them look out onto the front porch, which she enjoys.

When the weather is good, she spends a lot of time on that front porch. We worry that she may wander off, but usually we are there with her. However, I have on occasion driven up to the house and seen her sitting there all on her own...I think at a certain point we'll have to lock it down in the same way we have a locking system in her apartment, but so far we haven't had to confront the issue.

This room is definitely more of a living room than a family room, and that's because of the formality that Grandma loves so much. Growing up, this clearly would have been the room we kids "weren't supposed to go into." And the thing that is a constant surprise to me about this community living room is how much it actually gets used. In my old house, we rarely used our living room, but here it does get used. There are just a lot more people around in this house, and if my parents entertain friends, this is where they do it. And when Grandma hears people's voices coming from here, she'll come up and visit, which is how the community living room is contributing to Grandma living actively on a daily basis.

CHAPTER 11

THE DINING ROOM

The dining room has its own unique look for our meals. The first thing to understand is that we keep a tablecloth on our table at all times. "Back in the day," a tablecloth, and what you put on it - your dishes, serving pieces and silverware, were very important, it was one part of a larger statement about you and your family. And so the tablecloth was essential to my grandmother and my mother, and while less essential to me, I deferred to them.

Here's what happens with the tablecloth at meals: breakfast and lunch we put placemats on top of it, but come dinnertime, those are gone and the tablecloth stands alone. However, I think we're close to Grandma having a placemat at dinner, too. She needs something to help hold her plate better, and not slip around. When this happens, everyone will have placemats at dinner, too, so she doesn't feel like she's the odd one out. And while this won't be my Mom's preferred look for the table, she'll go along with it. This is the way of the 4-Gen Experiment, and it's fine, because it forces us to think about what is truly essential for each of us as individuals, as families and as one big family, and though it's not always easy, it's usually best.

What else is unique about our look in this room is that our placemats are always themed for the season. This is my mother's idea and it's a great plus for Grandma; they help orient her to the seasons and holidays, and without being told, Grandma has an understanding of where she is—timewise. It also ties in nicely with her "job" in the Dining Room: setting the table. Not only does this help our family run more smoothly, it also helps her brain function more smoothly, too (usually.) When Grandma's laying out the forks and knives, the plates and the placements, she's also cueing her brain. Her physical activity is driving her mental activity and she's realizing… *"It's time to eat."* The secondary benefit is that for this part of her day, she moves more fluidly with less agitation. When my mom prepares her lunch, and brings it to her in her apartment, Grandma's much more argumentative about whether she's eaten or not.

Another specific "look" to our dining room table is our centerpiece. Like our tablecloth, it's also something that we keep on the table all the time, and it's also related to the time of year. In the same way placemats cue Grandma and orient her in time, so do our centerpieces. Every time Grandma sees the centerpiece when she's setting, or clearing, the table, she's reminded of where we are in the calendar year. We'll have centerpieces for Halloween, Thanksgiving, Christmas, Valentine's Day, Easter. My mother will do a Fall centerpiece with pretty colored leaves, pine cones, and candles. She'll also do a Spring thing, too, but as soon as our fresh flowers bloom, they take over the main centerpieces. We live in Ohio and spring flowers, following our long winters, will always reign supreme. All around the outside of our house we have flowerbeds, and when they start coming into bloom, we cut them and bring them into the house. My mom always puts them in a vase on the table, and she also always brings a vase of flowers into Grandma's room.

During Spring, I have a large ceramic piece and in it are woven carrots, eggplants, cabbage, lettuce etc. It looks artistic, which I like aesthetically, but more important is that its artistry ensures that the fruit and vegetables DO NOT look like *real* fruit or vegetables. Meaning? Grandma's not biting into any fake food. I've seen this happen, and it doesn't end well. This is "cueing" in a generic sense. Food items like this cue Grandma into thinking, *"That's where I eat."* It's my little way of doing it here, but you could also have "cueing pieces" like art work on the walls.

Our visual environment plays such a big part in our understanding of our world. For people with Alzheimer's/Dementia, tying their surroundings of their present with what they knew, or grew up with in their past, helps them enormously. Grandma grew up in southern West Virginia in a town called Ghent (pron: Gent.) She had orchards of fruit trees, gardens filled with vegetables and pretty flowers everywhere. She and her parents, and her 8 brothers and sisters, always came together and sat down to family style meals full of food from their land—that's what she knew, that's what's familiar, and seeing aspects of that in our Dining Room cues her brain to think, *"Time to eat."* Though not complicated, it's surprising how these simple things help Grandma so much.

One thing we don't have is a china cabinet. However, it would be a good thing for Grandma, because as with the centerpieces and placemats, seeing the dishes would be subtle cueing to her brain that eating happens in this room.

Choosing which of our dining room tables to use was something of a problem, as too many choices make things a little tricky sometimes. My mom and dad had their large pedestal table that they were very fond of, and I had the table that was Grandma's that she gave me, which I loved. It was a Sears and Roebucks dining table from 1914 that cost $18.68 at the time, and it held so much history. For Grandma's generation, the dining room table was where the business of the family was done, where her brothers who returned from the war sat down and told their stories, and where life's dramas and hilarity all played out. Ultimately, that table just wasn't big enough for all of us, and it made me so sad that I couldn't use it. But that doesn't mean that we chose my mom's table, we didn't, and there was a lot of sadness on her part when she learned her table wasn't going to be a part of the 4-Gen Experiment. For her generation, it was a big deal to buy your first dining table, and she loved hers. The problem was that it was a pedestal table and it was just too unstable. You lean on things more and more as you get older, and when I tested her pedestal table by leaning on it, I could see how unstable it was. I ended up buying a table that was very sturdy, where you can stand up and can lean on it without worrying about the possible seesaw effect.

Around the table we have chairs chosen for their comfort level—they all have cushions, making them quite comfy for everyone, but they also work for another reason, too: their arms. Armchairs are important because they help when you are getting into, up and out of them, especially for the elderly. Using the chair's arms to hold onto and steady themselves is crucial. We have a couple of armchairs, and also a couple without arms, and we all make sure that Grandma always has an armchair. In the future, we might be swapping out some of the armless chairs for armchairs, and we're all good with that.

The rug I have in our Dining Room is very thin, to compensate for a potential walking/tripping/falling hazard, which unfortunately, rugs do bring. I've obsessed about making sure it's held down incredibly well. So underneath it is a very good rug holder, but you also could use rug tape, or Velcro. But it's really important to make sure there's not one single spot that someone can trip over, because you can be certain that if there is that *one* spot, your loved one will find it, will trip and will fall.

The majority of our lights are on dimmers in the Dining Room, but we make sure the light is bright enough so Grandma can see her plate and her food. Sometimes, my mom will want to have candles, and I'll say, *"Okay, great, but we still have to turn up the lights."*

This room is incredibly important to Grandma. She loves coming in and watching the birds that are flying around, or nesting, or feeding in our magnolia tree. It's an enormous tree, and Greg put four bird feeders out there, and I think that every single bird in the area comes to our house for the meal. Plus, there are big fat squirrels out there that Grandma finds very entertaining—she loves watching as they steal the birdfeed in feeders. But she not only watches the birds and the squirrels, sitting in the Dining Room allows her to make sure she catches us when we're leaving for the day.

I think it is a real challenge for there to be multiple women living in the same house, but we've made our way through the ups and downs so far: the kitchen is completely my mom's domain, and I defer to her in there. However she wants it to be arranged, it's arranged. Where I get to mandate things (most of the time) are those very functional elements: the dining room table, the silverware, the lighting. It may not be how any of us would do it in our "ideal" home, but we accept what we have and just deal with what we don't—sometimes the "dealing with" is done quietly, sometimes less so. But we do try to get to a place where even if we're not 100% happy with what we see, what we eat, and how we live, we understand the reason behind it, which seems to be the first step towards accepting it and thriving in the hive.

CHAPTER 12

THE KITCHEN

We live in a house that was built in 1914, and with it came its very small kitchen: cabinets, a sink, a refrigerator, a dishwasher; it's very compact, very utilitarian, and that's very fine with all of us.

When the 4-Gen Experiment was being discussed and designed, we decided that for as long as my mom, dad and grandma were living with us, we'd have a bigger dining room, than a kitchen. This decision has proven to be such a big part of our life; we cook in the kitchen, but we eat in the dining room. It's part of "purpose driven space," of which I'm a huge advocate—especially when it comes to seniors with Alzheimer's/Dementia. Just like I did in Grandma's apartment, I'm always trying to make it clear why she is somewhere. When there's less choice there's less confusion, and our kitchen has only one choice, one purpose: cooking. (Okay, maybe getting a glass of water, sneaking a snack later, and washing dishes.) But in our kitchen, there's no place for sitting, no television to watch, no comfy sofa for reading.

The kitchen of our "experiment" contains many cooks: me, Adellina, my mom and Grandma (sort of.) And that works well for us. *Usually.* Have I mentioned that my mom was the head cook at our high school? I loved it then. Loved seeing her in action, in her element, being the boss. And the upshot is that today she still has great pride in her kitchen, which includes its utensils, pots, pans, and all the "accoutrements" that go into making a kitchen work efficiently and aesthetically. And like everything else in our "experiment", it came with its own set of issues.

Issue #1: Whose flatware would we use?

Issue #2, 3, and 4: Whose plates, coffee cups and drinking glasses would we use?

The only thing I really cared about was *not* using Grandma's filigree flatware pieces from the 70s. More than aesthetics (well, it was some of that, too, because these were not my style at all!) but these pieces would just be too hard to clean. My wish in this one area? New flatware that was weighted really well. This would be especially important for Grandma, making it easier for her to grasp and hold onto. Also, I wanted whatever we chose to have big enough soupspoons because she likes her soup. Well-weighted flatware would help her eat well, and this is an ongoing concern for us, as it is with many people who care for loved ones with Alzheimer's/Dementia.

After the flatware issue was decided (and I got my way), I didn't care much about the rest. But my mom did. She cared a lot about the dishes we used, and so she pushed for, and got what she wanted in this area. The result has been great.

All of our dishes are Corelle. It's the original "break and chip resistant glass dinnerware." Think prison-ware in white. With its divided plate you can also think of it as a high-class TV dinner tray, but I guess that has a lot to do with how you define "high class." We all love these dishes for a number of reasons:

1. If Grandma drops a plate, it won't break and shatter, so she can use these and we don't have to worry.
2. The plates are divided, and like many of the decisions we made around the house, this one also helps Grandma to *not* be confused. Yes, plates can be confusing when you think of it like this: spicy flavors mixing together with salty flavors, sauces running into dressings, meat bumping into

vegetables, and to what end? Well, for Grandma, and others in the same state of mind, the end is a dinner plate full of food that has become too confusing and too choice driven. Though she's not at the point of turning away foods that touch, other people like her do exactly that, but these plates don't let that happen. Plus, from a dexterity standpoint, the lip on the plate assists her in small ways, too; it keeps sauces on the plate as opposed to heading off of it, and it makes it easier for Grandma to get her food onto her utensil.

3. The third thing, and this is important from the caregivers standpoint, Corelle is microwaveable.

4. Let's go back to the "break and chip resistant" element of our decision. This is great for Grandma's desire to help out and not be a burden. She has a job at mealtime: she's the one setting the table, and she does it with great precision that at times borders on fanaticism. I was taught how to set a table, but watching my Grandma do it with her great care and intention has made me re-think what I've been doing (think the opposite) for all these years prior to our "experiment." The great thing about our Corelle is that it stops us from freaking out when she's setting the table, as well as when she's doing her other kitchen "jobs," like helping to load and unload the dishwasher. By the way, she doesn't remember to do this unless the dishwasher is open. If it's closed, her brain doesn't register *there's something inside,* or *something outside that needs to be inside.* This is actually helpful to us in the kitchen, as it eliminates some of the worry about her getting into "trouble." Take our pantry, for instance.

Off the kitchen, we have a little breakfast room, in it is a pantry, and in that pantry is where I put all the spices, vitamins and usual pantry-type items: crackers, chips, soups to nuts. What I didn't want to happen was for Grandma to open it up and take out cayenne pepper thinking it was paprika, then add it to something. Those results wouldn't be good for her, or anyone. But because the pantry is *not* in plain sight of the kitchen area, her mind "reads" it as *Oh, I don't have it.* And if she's in the breakfast room, but the doors to the pantry are closed, her mind "reads" it, as *There's nothing there.*

Knowing how Grandma's mind reads things helps us a lot. It helps her too, because she is able to be more autonomous in the kitchen, which she wants and we want for her. It's not like she does that much on her own, but she might be making a cheese sandwich, having a piece of fruit with some crackers and cheese, which she'll fix for herself, or sneaking anything sweet! But since we understand how her brain is currently working, we can let her keep doing the things that make her happy. Even when she's in there with someone else, helping doing food prep… and at 94, even with her issues, Grandma's still good at things like cleaning green beans, peeling potatoes, stirring the cake batter, peeling the eggs. And since she is, we ask her to do them, and she stays engaged in her life and ours, too.

In terms of the actual cooking, she isn't doing this at all. She isn't using our gas stove, so right now this is a non-issue, but it might change to an actual issue in the future. And like other things, we try to stay ahead of this by having a plan. Here that plan is getting an automatic shut-off. All we'll have to do is flip a master-switch, which will allow the stove to operate. So anyone that's cognitive, would know, *"Oh, I have to flip that switch to get this working."* But if you're not cognitive, like Grandma, you wouldn't know to do this, so you wouldn't be able to use the stove, so the risk of a disaster is eradicated. And then there's something called, "Fire Avert" (Auto Safety Stove Off) from Shark Tank. This is designed for electric stoves and is around $150. You plug it into the outlet, and then you plug the stove into it, when your smoke alarm sounds, Fire Avert hears it and automatically shuts off the electric stove.

What else we're trying to stay ahead of in the kitchen is scalding water. Doing this was fairly easy: we put a temperature control on our faucets. Now for Grandma's safety this was great, but for my happiness, this was less than great, and it was a tricky thing in our little "experiment." I love having hot water come out of the faucets. I love it when I'm washing dishes, love it when I'm washing pots and pans. In my old house we accommodated this passion/quirk of mine with a very high water temp setting. But of course I didn't want Grandma to get scalded when she was just washing off her plate, or getting a glass of water. So "we" found a simple solution: "we" got an electric teapot. It heats up the water really fast and very hot, which I use for washing up my pots and pans. But Grandma *doesn't* use it and so she stays safe.

Interestingly, this has helped my mother's health problems, too. For years, her pot and pan cleaning method went like this: scrub like a maniac for 15 or 20 minutes with a steel wool pad. Clearly, this was not great for a woman with shoulder and back issues. Now, she simply uses boiling water to help her clean. Little things like this really help her body feel better at the end of the day.

I know what you're thinking about. It's that elephant in the kitchen of all Alzheimer's/Dementia seniors, right? That scary knife-wielding elephant! Yes, what about the knives? How do you keep Grandma away from them? And here's something that might surprise you: I still have our knives out. They're in a block, all there tucked away in their tidy designated slots. And that block is away from, and not anywhere near, the silverware drawer. Yes, there are knives in that drawer, but of the butter knife variety...not much danger in those, I think. But if the situation occurs when I'm proven wrong, I'll put those away, too. But I know her well, and I know that she's not a depression risk, so I doubt she'll do anything harmful to herself. Plus, as I mentioned above, she no longer makes any food where she needs to use a sharp knife.

And then there's this little piece of Cini honesty: I actively spy on Grandma. So while I'm not bubble wrapping her, and/or my house, I am noticing what she's doing, and where she is now in her mental acuity, or lack thereof. From these *observations,* I'm making adjustments, which just means that I'm trying to manage the situation, but not make it a TSA security deal.

I'm carefully watching the knife situation, again, trying to stay ahead of it, and if we need to make changes, I've thought about what we'll do: get a magnetic strip, and mount it underneath the cabinet, close to the stove where we use them. That magnetic strip is really strong and will hold the knives beautifully. But Grandma won't see them at that height because she only sees things at her eye level. And while I can also put them all in a locked drawer, I'd rather have the knives near for when the rest of us cook. With Grandma's "out of sight and out of mind" mentality, I think we'll be fine.

Small adjustments have surprising impact in the kitchen. We still have glassware, meaning actual glass, even though Grandma is a little shaky. But we switched to *thick* glassware. It's heavier in weight, and because of its etched design, there's enough texture to make it easier for her to grip. One change we also made was in the size of the glasses we use. We bought smaller glasses so that Grandma could hold them more easily, and carry them with less trouble. Besides, she's not from the "Big Gulp" guzzler generation, so a smaller glass is completely normal for her.

Being the lady she was, and still is, Grandma has a specific type of coffee cup she likes, and it's not a big heavy mug; it's a very delicate, thin bone china cup. Unfortunately, she's having trouble keeping it upright these days, and she's starting to let it tip a little more and more. But as I said, she likes that ladylike cup a lot, so I can see where this is going. But what am I going to do? I want her to be independent, but I don't want her to spill all the time and feel bad about that. What are our options? We're getting close to having to figure this out.

I've saved the best for last, our refrigerator, where, organization is key, but not because I'm trying to be a control freak. It's similar to the Corelle divided plates: trying hard to keep everything separate, so it's easier for Grandma to understand. So cheese has to be in the cheese drawer, meats in the meat drawer, green "leafys" in the vegetable bin, and condiments, well, let's take a moment to address them because in our household...condiments are king, and they reign supreme. They can also quickly become overwhelming and confusing. So we're constantly going through them, and paring them down—or at least trying to. If you eat at home a lot, which we do, you really do tend to have more than you think in the condiment department.

It's not just the constant paring down that's essential, it's also the constant need to keep the refrigerator organized, and to keep it functional. This is especially important for Grandma who, these days, takes something out and doesn't always remember to put it back in. And on the occasion that she does, it's hit or miss if it's going to end up in the right place. It's not that I care, it's that I just want her to be able to find what she needs the next time. Again, this is all about keeping her independent as long as possible. If she opens the door to the fridge and sees so many things and has so many choices, she will probably close the door quickly. But if it's clear and organized—she'll make a choice. She'll take care of herself a little more. She'll be able to make herself a sandwich, take out a hardboiled egg and eat that with some cheese and crackers, and for a little bit longer, she'll feel like she's not being a burden.

CHAPTER 13

COMMUNITY FAMILY ROOM

Walking into our Community Family Room for the first time, you'd probably be struck by a single thought: *"Whoa, there's a lot of seating in this room."* And you'd be right---sort of. We don't just have a lot--we have an *excessive* amount of seating in here.

Any designer coming to my house would be horrified, I know I am, but more than style dictating my design of this room, one question did: *"How do I get four generations, plus any number of additional folks, into one room and make it comfortable to everyone?"* The answer is seen in the three sofas, lounge chair and multiple ottomans. Yes, essentially I designed a family-room-meets-frathouse. And much to my dismay, yet also to my delight, it works. Here's what I mean.

Frat houses are really set up so that a large number of people can come over and hang out; it matters less about how the room looks and more about how everyone there has somewhere to sit. And so we've got our two large sofas and our love seat. And then we've got our oversized lounge chair and just for good measure we've got our four kinds of ottomans. So you can see what I mean about it being awful, but you can also, hopefully, see what I mean about it being a space where everybody can come together, hang out, be comfortable, and have a good seat to watch a movie or just talk. And in Grandma's case, sometimes just sit here and be with us.

For me, a family room should be a place where our bodies relax; it's where we're able to talk to someone, watch something, fall asleep wherever we find ourselves seated, and sometimes just sit and watch the fire burning in the fireplace. It's different in that way to a dining room or living room; those rooms are more intentional. A living room is where you greet and entertain guests who aren't your family. But in your family room, you don't just put on your comfortable clothes, you also put on your comfortable "face," this is the room where you let your hair down. In the living room you've got your "candy dishes," in the family room you've got your snacks. This is the place for BBQ potato chips and everything that goes along with them. The upholstery colors here are richer and darker, the better to hide soiling (from those BBQ chips and fixings), and it has a more masculine feel to it than the living room.

This room is the hub of our socializing, and with the exception of all of us eating in the dining room, this is where we all come together. It's an unspoken understanding in the "Social Experiment" that if you want to be alone, you better be in another place…you lose that right when you enter this room. And while today I think this is a good thing for everyone, it took some time getting used to.

At the very beginning, Grandma and my parents felt a little hesitant to use the big Community Family Room. They felt more that their private rooms were their family rooms. Mom and Dad had their den upstairs with its TV and recliners, and Grandma had her sitting room with its own TV, couch, and reclining chair. If my Dad and I were sitting in this room, and we were alone and then others came in, he'd say, *"Okay, you watch whatever you want, I'll go upstairs,"* and I'd feel bad and say, *"You don't need to leave."* But over time we all got used to being together, and little by little we started using the space as "everyone's" space. We're all sensitive to who's in there; when the kids are home and in there with their friends, we'll give them their space---like normal Parents and Grandparents. What also helped us was establishing "family viewing rules." I.e. when the show gets going, we stop talking. While it might sound obvious or maybe silly, rules like this make a difference in everyone feeling welcome and happy in this space.

Having a room where everyone feels comfortable and gets along has another great benefit: it helps create a real sense of community. Sometimes in homes, a teenager lays claim to a basement and no one's allowed to go there, or a guy's got his a man cave-- with emphasis on the word "*his*." In other households, someone's got their "chair." With us, that doesn't exist, here we've created our own little democracy. No one owns a specific seat in this room, and what that means for our family is that we all see it as a community cooperation space. (Of course, if Grandma comes in and all the seats are taken, someone will always give up a seat to her, because there's a degree of respect for a senior.) But no one gets terribly upset because no one's territorial. Finding this level of community understanding is important for the success of our 4-Gen Experiment, so if seating *is* important to your family, then it's important to define that seating plan or hierarchy. As with most things, once again, it's about a family communicating clearly, openly and with respect for each other's feelings and opinions.

We've designed the Community Family Room in a way that works for us as individuals and as family: the lights are on a dimmer, which is good because this is the kind of room you can snuggle down in. And if someone falls asleep, or in my Dad's case... *when* he falls asleep, I can go in and dim the lights so he can sleep well, but not hurt himself when he gets up. We put up blackout curtains in here, too, which is great for watching movies. Our flooring is a mix: some hard wood, an area rug, and some carpet.

We also have a fireplace in here. I love fires, we all do, and we're not worried about Grandma being around it. She never comes up to it or bothers with it. She'll say it's "pretty" and it's "nice," but she doesn't engage with it, and it's not something her curiosity causes her to mess with. It's one of those issues, though, where you really have to know who you're dealing with, and I know Grandma isn't a fire gal and so she's safe.

This is a multilevel room, and not by my design, but rather by a '70s remodel that was done prior to our moving in. But the couple of steps work well for how our family uses this room. When we're watching movies, it's our own version of stadium seating. And it serves as seating for all the kids when we have a lot of people over, and we like having a lot of people over. This is the room where we have our big family Christmas tree, (Grandma, and Mom and Dad have their own small ones in their own private suites) and other holidays and parties find us in here, too.

The steps create an interesting issue for the Social Experiment in the way they pertain to Grandma. She can access the Community Family Room from her suite without traversing steps, however, she can only access half of this room. In order to access the other side she has to go up two steps that do not have a railing, and this proves more difficult for her. One of us now jumps up and helps her; this is a new development and I'm about a day away from installing a hand rail here. She's fine, however, on the other set of steps that takes her from the Community Family Room to the kitchen or bathroom, because those steps have a railing. It's not an issue to hold her hand on the stairs. I like to do that, most of us do, and she likes the physical contact, but the issue is this: what happens when no one's there? Then what? At that point it could become a safety issue, because the thing about Grandma is that she doesn't avoid these stairs. When she wants to go somewhere, she goes, and nothing stops her, and so we'll need to make it safe for her and allow her to maintain her independence.

This is a good example of how we've designed our social experiment in relation to Grandma: we didn't try to work through everything immediately. Our mindset was to take it as it goes, and this has helped us to not become overwhelmed by what's happening. It's a simple idea: go through the house and see what works and what doesn't. To do that, we approached Grandma's needs using a model we'd already gone through twice and with good success with: childproofing. Back then, we saw what we *absolutely* needed to do to keep the kids safe, and addressed that first. It's like that here, too, with Grandma. Certain things weren't issues at the beginning and so we waited; it's easy to add. Not only does this help us to be less overwhelmed, it also helps Grandma to hold onto her dignity a little longer.

The Community Family Room also helped me achieve one of my design goals for Grandma. I wanted her to have to pass through this room, and engage with us. Physically, her apartment is off the Community Family Room, and opens up into it. And we *want* Grandma to engage with us. Some nights we'll ask her to come watch TV with us and she will, other nights she'll opt out, but it's still an opportunity for us to have even a brief conversation with her. And that's a good thing. There are times that I might only get five minutes with her, but it's still five minutes that we both like to have. If she were in a nursing home or senior living facility we wouldn't get that. For her, even those brief conversations are helpful. I think the continuity of the relationships she has with all of us she sees every day lets her be more clearheaded, and more lucid. With others who aren't there all the time, she sometimes struggles to place them, and is confused.

Here's the funny thing about this over furnished, frat room from the 70s: people love it! It makes them happy. And when it comes down to it, isn't that what a family room is all about? How many great interiors do you remember from growing up? Probably not many, but how many great times do you remember? And I bet you remember where they took place…not so much because of the room's design aesthetic, but because of its comfort, the company and the conversation.

CHAPTER 14

THE PARENTS' BEDROOM

It's been over two years since my parents moved in and this 4-Gen Social Experiment began. And just to recap where we were right before they moved in: they were concerned, incredibly concerned, about the stairs. You might remember that twice I caught them measuring the stair height, and twice counting the actual number of stairs. You might also recall that it was because they were absolutely convinced my stairs were higher and there were more of them than theirs. Both turned out to be not true, everything was exactly the same.

What was true though, was that my parents thought they'd be spending these years of their life living in a ranch house. And when they learned that wasn't happening, and that instead they'd be living with us, they accepted it. And once they accepted that, they assumed they'd be living on the ground floor. And when that hope was dashed because Grandma was getting the downstairs apartment and they accepted that, too, they played their last card: "We'll convince Lisa that the stairs are higher and there's just too many of them." And when that was proven false, up they went.

Well, I guess every cloud does truly have a silver lining because now they're up and around, and walking the dog every night for a half hour to an hour. Whether it's by choice or from being forced upon them doesn't really matter, what does matter is that this behavior is a complete 180 from when they moved in. And so it dawned on me that had I let them win on that step issue, their physical health would have continued to downgrade. But getting to this newfound good health wasn't necessarily easy.

My grandmother and my father have had both knees replaced. My mother has also had both knees replaced and also shoulder and back surgery. In the first several weeks after moving in, the noises that came out of her when she was on those steps were just awful: groans that rocked the roof, grunts that shook the foundation. I thought for sure our little Social Experiment was going to be a complete failure. Every night I'd lie awake, my mind making countless design plans, asking myself "Could we reconfigure the downstairs to accommodate yet another full bedroom suite?" (I'd also lie awake pondering this question, too: "Have I lost my mind completely thinking this could work?") My great support for my mother during this phase amounted to saying; "Just consider it like physical therapy, Mom." And that was another reason I thought our Social Experiment would fail: consoling and comforting clearly is not my strongpoint. But several weeks later, I noticed she wasn't making as much noise going up and down. And soon after that, I noticed another shift in her behavior: she was going up and down a lot more.

When they first moved in, it was clear that my mom was making very conscious decisions about getting everything done downstairs before heading upstairs, and staying up there for the rest of the night. Then that changed. And now, up and down she goes—all day long and into the night. Today, she and my dad both see the benefit of not being stagnant, of not being in front of the TV. It feels good to them, good to be outside enjoying their dog walks, good because they get to enjoy a little private time, too... just the two of them on their own. As you can see, the Social Experiment is a rather community oriented affair with private time being a rather rare commodity. So with their newfound improved health, and a dog that needs a lot of walking, they now take nice long walks, through their nice neighborhood, talking to a lot of nice neighbors.

Their intellectual health has also benefitted from the social experiment. They've told us that with us coming in and out, and when the kids come home and the constant parade of their friends coming in and out, they're "keeping young." Their daily multigenerational conversations about what's going on in the world, keeps them engaged. And technology isn't passing them by either: my mom Snapchats with Addie in Italy, and Grandma Vibers (like Skype or Facetime) with Jake in California, with no problem whatsoever. If we weren't with them, I wonder if they'd be so interested in making the effort with technology, but we are here and they do make the effort.

And all of this lies just 16 standard height stairs away from their upstairs bedroom suite.

You enter their suite, which includes a den, bedroom and full bathroom, through a door to their den, which is off the main hallway. They have 3 recliners in there: one for each of them, and a guest. And they do have guests. When my kids are home, or their other grandchildren are over, they all like to go up and spend time in the den, whether they're watching television or just hanging out together, it seems that everyone feels comfortable up there.

The den is also home to a very beautiful coffee table. Which also happens to be a very large coffee table; it's a piece of furniture that my dad really loves. They didn't bring a lot of furniture over from their old house, but this one made it. It's placement-- in front of the fireplace-- means the fireplace is no longer used. But my dad likes to see the coffee table, and when he does, it makes him happy, and that speaks louder than a working fireplace.

Moving from the den into the bedroom...there is a full sized bed, a nightstand, dresser and TV. The room is not big, but it's closer to the bathroom, and they like it. Plus, they made the choice themselves. When I was designing their suite, I gave them the options: 1. Have the den be the bigger room and the bedroom be smaller or, 2. Let the bedroom be the larger space. They chose option 1. And though they said it's more convenient for them to be closer to the bathroom (and it is), part of me wonders if it was also just a little bit about them being able to make their own choice, and not having to agree with me. (It was obvious that I was pushing for the larger room to become the bedroom).

The bathroom (which used to be a laundry room) has a roll-in shower with a seat, and two sink cabinets, one for each of them, which I felt was important. In their last house, they had separate bathrooms, and now they're sharing one, another adjustment they've been forced to make. And so, giving them each their own little space and a little more control over their environment, I hoped would ease their transition into our house, and help make settling in less stressful.

A big challenge we encountered was what to do with the washer/dryer once we'd decided to take the laundry room and turn it into their bathroom? We came up with a solution that is possibly the best one in the whole house (other than putting the big thermometer outside the dining room for Grandma to look at and report on throughout the day.) In the same hallway that leads to Greg and my bedroom and also adjoins their bathroom, we put a stackable washer dryer. Pocket doors let them have access to it from their bathroom, while the rest of us access it from the hallway. One little trick made the whole plan a phenomenal success: locks on the pocket doors. Making it impossible for anyone to enter the other spaces unannounced.

Off their bathroom is a door that leads outside to a flat porch. Greg put a railing around it and rubber brick pavers for drainage, and once the functional purpose was handled, some aesthetic choices were made for out there, too. We put out pretty pots and put equally pretty plants in them, and then we added nice outdoor furniture. They can, and they do, sit out there with their morning coffee… weather and temperatures permitting. Getting their coffee ready in the AM is part of my mother's morning ritual. She does this for

Grandma and for them, and it's a good thing she mastered those stairs, because the other part of her AM ritual is delivering the coffee she's made, upstairs to my dad. It's nice to see Mom having coffee with Dad out there in the mornings, sitting in their robes, getting fresh air and starting their day, together.

As much as they've settled in upstairs, and as much as I think they like it, I also think when Grandma's gone, they will run down and take over that space. It's so much more private. Sometimes they, and Greg and I, and the kids, and Grandma all have a need for privacy! But while I know that is true, I also know something else is true, too. It's what lies at the very foundation of this experiment, and it's what's changed my attitude about thinking everything needs to be perfect, and stopped me from worrying that someone will get hurt. And this is it: knowing that Grandma, and Mom and Dad, will be happier living at home than in a senior living home. This truth has freed me, that no matter how beautiful I would design it, it's about connection, freedom and ultimately LOVE. LOVE with a little bit of common sense and knowledge is better than all the state of the art facilities in the world; it's about quality of life vs. ultimate safety and perfection.

CHAPTER 15

COMING OUT OF THE CLOSET

What exactly is private? And what is public? Is there a line somewhere between the two, and if so, is it drawn with an impermeable marker, like a big fat Sharpie, or is it drawn in faint pencil, with an eraser ready on top? These are questions that come into play with our 4-Gen Experiment, and they continue to be tricky ones for us.

At first glance, the idea of privacy didn't seem like it would be so tricky, or complicated, or delicate. But what I've realized with this generational living arrangement of ours, is that what's none of those things for me is often exactly that for our other generations. And if it was ever true, it is here. But of course, not in the way I thought it would be.

I figured our issues would be centered around the bedroom, bathroom, or talking on the phone. Clear and simple, right? Where it *did* show up left me totally unprepared, and that was in our stuff - our physical and stored stuff, our keepsakes and private histories.

Maybe a *large* part of the reason is that with Grandma's, and Mom and Dad's generations, certain things were simply never discussed. You never asked what someone's income was, how old someone was, or what was their religion. These things, and others, too, were deemed "inappropriate." In their days, a different, and broader, respect for other people's private lives was observed.

What's private to my grandmother is a longer list much more than what's private to my parents. Likewise, what's private to my parents is definitely a longer list than what it is to Greg and me. And my kids? For sure, they're even less private than any of the rest of us, and they really have a hard time understanding our concepts of privacy. I wonder if the kids think *You're old and you're an open book, you can't have any more secrets?* Maybe so. I wonder whether they see all of our things as some kind of an ongoing archeological dig. Supporting that line of thinking is Addie's choice of major in college: archeology. I'm not surprised, nor did my "apple" fall too far, either from her tree.

As a kid, I remember going to my grandparents' houses and racing right up to their attics' to scavenge through their histories. My siblings and I didn't ask for permission, we figured if it was in storage boxes it was fair game. They were "old," they were "open books," what "secrets" did they have? Looking back now after my dealings with the 4-Gen Experiment, I know that none of this was "fair game," that their storage was very private to them, and held, and still holds, some of their deepest and most personal memories. But back then, the excitement of possibly finding an old prom dress, costume jewelry, old photographs and newspaper clippings, even a tiny old Singer sewing machine, trumped all thoughts of privacy.

In her youth, Grandma was a real adventurer. She and Grandpa took a year off in their 50s and traveled all over the U.S. Up in their West Virginia attic were incredible "artifacts" from that trip: turquoise from Arizona, a stone with garnets in it from Wyoming, blankets from native American tribes etc. My other grandparents, Italian/German immigrants, didn't travel much, but they liked to store things in their attic. Up there they had cedar chests and steamer trunks full of things: furniture, dresses, hats, old shoes--the gamut! This was the generation that didn't throw anything away.

And then we moved in together, and the question of what to do with all the years of individual and family's private keepsakes and documents, their furniture and kitchen supplies, and all the holiday and seasonal decorations, became a pressing concern.

Looking back, boundaries should have been set early on. But instead, we forged ahead. We thought that creating individual attic storage spaces, one above Mom and Dad's suite, and another one above Grandma's apartment, would work out just fine. When that wasn't quite enough, we also gave Mom and Dad additional space in the garage attic, pool house attic and finally in the basement. The basement is the one that continues to be the source of the most friction, because it's the space that we all have the most access to. Everyone's always down there, and rarely do we put things away, at least not in the timeliest of manners. Plus, there's our constant negotiating for space down there. But what's really the hardest for the older two generations is this: we get into each other's private things.

For me, one of the hardest parts concerned something else. In the basement, we have a file cabinet full of documents: wills, birth certificates, death certificates, banking statements, financial information, and private items like love letters and photographs. We don't want everyone to see these, but what are we to do with them? Hide them underneath our beds like we did when we kept diaries at 13? Stick them in shoeboxes we store away on a top closet shelf, under a few old sweaters, like we did with our love letters at 15? My problem is that I'm in charge of these most sacred documents, the keeper of our collective history, and in assuming this (unrequested) position, I became cognizant of what keeping these things meant to them: a way for them to pass on who they were to future generations. It's a responsibility that stressed me out completely. Of course, I didn't have a chance to scan anything, and so the idea that if there was a fire, our whole history would be gone, kept me up at night. Then I bought a fireproof box to keep it all safe. One challenge taken care of. And that was a big relief. Until the next one came along and reared up: personal mementos and holiday decorations.

Once again, the 4-Gen experiment took me by surprise. This time it was by Mom's generation, the Better Homes and Gardens crowd, the Betty Crocker girls, and their fierce attachment to their… decorations. While I didn't then, I now understand why, where I see simple "decorations," Mom's generation sees the story of who they are: as a family and as religious people, as well as how classy they are and what values they hold. In both Grandma's and Mom's day, being a homemaker was highly esteemed, and how you did your decorations was a representation of what kind of person, mother, wife, and homemaker you were. It was a reflection on them personally, in almost the same way their kids were. Knowing this, you can probably see that it was a big deal for my Mom's decorations to have their own place separate from mine. And I had to learn to become more respectful of the meaning they held to her.

But respect was one thing, and space was another. I was plagued with the question of, *"Where was it all to go?"* (Along with the special holiday punch bowl, the deviled egg plate and a lot of things from Mom's kitchen.) Then we found a space! It was under the basement stairs, had shelves and a door, and though it looked like it might have been built to hold canned foods (enough for a small Armageddon), we knew it would be perfect for all the things Mom doesn't get into all the time, but feels naked without. And voila, what was once an extra area under the steps is now a full on storage unit. In addition to its shelving, to this truly gloriously functional storage area was added a metal shelf on wheels! Mom puts her stuff on it, rolls it out and around with ease, gets to her other things, and then rolls it back in with just as much ease. And she's really happy with that. What she was also happy with was that the space has a door that she can close and other people (meaning all of us) won't add to her storage or rearrange it.

Grandma is another story. She doesn't do any real cooking, so she was fine about not having her things, but photos are so important to her. We made sure there was room for her to keep them around or hang them up in her room. The other things she values, and has sentimental attachments to, are things we keep out in our public spaces for her to see all the time, and this is particularly comforting to her. We have a toothpick holder that her father made out of the wood of a curly maple tree, as well as the table he made that the family bible sits on; Grandma brought that with her from her home, too.

Grandma's past thinking about the other things she gave up in the move in with us. She's at the point now that if something isn't right in front of her to see, it doesn't exist for her. It's sad, but also easier on her, because she doesn't get upset or agitated if she doesn't see something she might have had at another time in her life. And yet, regardless of that, and adding to my craziness, is this: Grandma *still* has her own Christmas decorations!

If you're considering doing a multi-gen thing for yourself, I'd suggest some things I wish someone had suggested for me. They're not that complicated, but they save complications occurring later on.

1. Consider having everyone's storage in separate locations, if possible. This way you don't have to worry about mixing anything up.

2. If there's not a lot of space, the next best idea is this: be a better organizer than I am. Knowing yourself, and the others in your family mix, helps, too. I know we don't store things particularly well, so I hired an organizer for my own stuff, and that was so helpful. I should have insisted that Mom and Dad and Grandma hired her too.

3. Packing is a pain to begin with--it's arduous, and emotional, but there are things you can do to make it easier. If you don't have it in your budget to hire a person to help you organize, go to Target, Staples or Wal-Mart and buy different color bins for each person/family/kid. Had I done this I would have lessened our frustration level enormously. Here's what

I would have done: #1. Get bins with tops that snap in and have a handle on each side to make them easy to carry. #2. Don't get the ones that are big or great big. If there's a choice between a great big bin vs. two smaller ones, opt for the two smaller ones. When my father carries those giant ones up and down the steps from the basement or to the attic, I'm nervous like a crazy person. Even though we tell him we'll do it for him, he wants to be independent and not rely on us, which really is a good thing, and one that I respect. (I just wish it wasn't happening around lots of stairs.) Carrying smaller bins is much easier than larger ones, and the weight is less.

4. Schedule garage sales and/or call charitable organization for pick-ups. A local Veterans group or some other charity you like will often pick up your stuff. We didn't do this. And guess what? After we moved, we never did it either. So now, all of our stuff came into the house, and it has gotten awfully comfy where it's living and I fear it will never leave.

5. Craig's List/EBay: Our family's older generations are nervous about having people come into the house and looking around. *"Maybe they're staking the home out?" "Maybe they'll tie us up and mug us."* But our generation and the kids' are different, with a different set of ideas. If this appeals to you, definitely sell things on these sites.

6. Make their items very accessible and easy for them to get to on their own. We just put them in spots when they moved in, not in well-thought out spots. We also made the bad move of putting them in our garage attic, which isn't attached. Now they have to go out and sort through things where it's not convenient, and in all kinds of weather. Not so smart. A little space planning would have been a great thing—this from the interior designer!

7. For the men: whose lawnmower do you keep? Whose snow blower? Whose shovels and tools? These are all full of a

man's pride. If he bought a John Deere lawnmower, it was a really big deal and now you're saying get rid of it. It's these tiny taking away of things that someone has earned, or feels they have, that creates such resistance. And when those things are full of memories and may have defined who they were, that makes it even harder. That's what the older generation is thinking about at this age, and there has to be careful and respectful discussions about those objects and items. We should have scheduled time to sit down and have them.

I wish I had anticipated more of what could possibly cause a problem. I wish I had understood the difference between what they feel comfortable talking about vs. what we do. I wish I realized what they hold as private is likely what we deem public. Had I understood these things, I think I would have been able to lessen a lot of our angst and anxiety. If I had gone in with an awareness of possibly needing to have these tricky conversations, I'd have been so much more ready for them when they arose. (And absolutely delighted if they didn't!)

CHAPTER 16

WATCHING FOR CLUES

Grandma's always been a big lover of games, and playing them was always a big part of life in the 4-Generation Experiment. When my parents and grandmother were at their old house, we'd go over and spend time together playing games as a family. We played Uno, the Name game, Checkers and did jigsaw puzzles, too. Grandma always participated. She was competitive, liked to win for sure, but also just liked being a part of the fun.

So when we started noticing that each time we went around and the game came back to Grandma and she'd forgotten the rules, we started realizing something was up. She was still funny and more important, she was still having fun, but there was definitely something different about her.

Sometimes these clues turn up in expected places…like, fittingly, in a game of Clue.

CHAPTER 17

ADDED VALUE

Part of our job as family members, who love Grandma, is trying to find ways for her to be needed. Because the truth is, at this stage in her dementia, Grandma still *can* help. She can peel potatoes. She can fold the clothes. She can clean green beans and she can set the table. When she complained that a job was "too hard", that she "couldn't bend down," we didn't say, "Then, don't do it," we figured out a new way for her to complete the job. Now we place everything on the couch, she sits down next to the pile of clothes, and folds them. Everyone's happy with her efforts because she folds everything precisely and beautifully, but more importantly, Grandma is happy. She has a purpose, she's participating, she's contributing.

No one feels good when they only take and don't give back. And there are other ways Grandma gives back, too, ways we didn't plan, but that we started noticing. Through all of our busy lives in the house, it's grandma who will let the dog out and let her back in, and she does it far more than all of us do. She's more observant than we are in this area. As for our dog? Callie doesn't care that grandma has Alzheimer's. And if Grandma's having a good day or a bad day, Callie treats her just the same: when she wants to go out she'll whine and pester Grandma until she gets up and lets her out.

Interestingly, Grandma is always the one who notices when to let Callie back in, too.

The times Grandma reaches her limit and throws a fit over something, like she did over having to fold too much laundry, and bend over too low, well that's actually okay with us, too! We're winning the game here: she's alive and she's participating. This is about being needed, and that's when she feels the most alive. And I don't think that's different for any of us.

Chapter 18

Boundaries

There are three families living around here, but we don't always have to be all as one.

We can also be our own individual selves, having our own interactions, dealing with our own issues, enjoying our own private times. And sometimes we all have to remember that.

Having well defined spaces helps everyone to be comfortable, and there's another benefit, too: it's a way for us to understand and respect each other's privacy.

I don't (*usually*) barge into my parents' den, bathroom and bedroom apartment suite. I want to be sure that those areas remain their own private spaces. I try to do that with grandma, too; if she's in there sleeping, I won't go in, just as I wouldn't want her to come into my room unannounced. If I hear her stirring, I might peek in and see what she's up to, and then I'll knock, giving her the opportunity to make a decision about her own life, to let her say, "*Come in,*" or say nothing, in which case I won't go in.

Saturdays, are when I tend to be a little selfish about my time with Grandma. I usually go into her apartment and sit with her as we drink our coffees and watch TV. She'll ask me how my job is, and she likes to hear my answer. She'll ask me how the kids are, and likes to hear about them, too.

It's my time to spend with her. Talking to her and connecting with her in this way, in her private little suite of rooms, makes me realize that despite all the ongoing tweaks that our Social Experiment requires of us, it's absolutely worth it.

CHAPTER 19

GRANDMA'S SONG

The front porch is vintage Americana. For generations, families have sat on their front porch (weather permitting) waving to neighbors, and chatting with each other about life's events. A porch swing and rocking chairs soothed the soul, while lemonade quenched the body.

Our porch is a bit different. We have the swing and the rocking chairs and sometimes even the lemonade. So, you might wonder what is different? It's the porch song. We have a "song" that gets sung over and over every time Grandma is out on the porch.

While not a song with a real melody, it's song-like because of its very real chorus, which goes something like this "*That tree needs to be trimmed, but you'll need a professional to do it. It's hanging over the road too, someone's going to have to call the city."*

Then we break back into the song of normal conversation, sharing the news of work, family, fun and more.

And then the chorus starts again…. "*That tree needs to be trimmed, but you'll need a professional to do it. It's hanging over the road too, someone's going to have to call the city."*

Once again we agree, and once again we return to our conversation.

A minute or two later the chorus starts again…. "*That tree needs to be trimmed, but you'll need a professional to do it. It's hanging over the road too, someone's going to have to call the city.*"

This "song" gets played the entire time Grandma is on the porch. She may add how wonderful the day is, or how this is the nicest house Greg and I have ever had, but she'll always return to her chorus.

The reason why I call it a "song" is that I needed a way to look at the situation differently, so that I would not get irritated when Grandma stated the same information over and over again. When you listen to a song, and its chorus plays over and over, you don't get angry about it. It actually creates predictability and a place to rest your mind in between the new verses. Once I decided that Grandma repeating herself was the chorus to our conversation, my whole perspective changed. I didn't mind the repetition and would just answer her, again and again—and now with a smile vs. a smirk.

If you find yourself in this situation, try using this mind hack and turning the repeated question into a chorus in your mind, and just smile and sing along.

Chapter 20

"Just in Case"

My mom's in charge of the shopping. Seems like an easy sentence to write and to read, except that she shops like the Cold War is still going on and the Apocalypse is around the corner.

Which means that every two months, I go through an exercise and into the 'frig I go. It's about "consolidating." It's my response to my mom saying, *"We don't have any room in the refrigerator for this, or that."* In I go, chucking out multiple mustards, many mayonnaises, numerous miracle whips… along with the armies of relishes, pickles and ketchups. And always respecting Mom's big concern over expiration dates. And while she might be right about that issue, I wonder how it's helping us having to sort out 9 jars of black olives in the cupboard *("just in case"),* 7 tins of canned chicken, 18 cans of corn, 15 cans of green beans alongside them *"as a backup"*), and canned peas to last us 12 years for a *("what if?").* She buys for the pending revolution, or the blizzard that didn't happen then.

Some of the things that I have come to understand are that, not only did my mother raise five kids and bought for all of us, plus friends, but she grew up in the Cold War era. My grandmother and my father's parents both lived through the Depression Era, and so my parents were brought up with the thought in the back of their head that you never know what could happen tomorrow, and you should always be prepared, especially when it came to food.

The first week of our 4Gen experiment, my daughter opened the pantry cabinets and said, *"It's magic! There is actually food in here!"* She certainly saw my mother's doomsday prepping as a huge positive vs. my minimalist approach.

We have all learned to compromise. Our family (Greg and Me and our Kids) does not "do" snacks, chips, soft drinks nor sugar drinks. You would be surprised how much space these items take up in the fridge and cupboards. We're more of the avocado, banana, water crowd.

My mother has tried increasing the fresh food category in her shopping, which is greatly appreciated. But fresh avocados don't keep like a can of olives, and so she's constantly adjusting, trying not to buy as much, so we don't have to give so much away to the wildlife in the yard because it went bad.

My senior living design experience helps a bit in understanding how your sense of taste changes as you age. Some seniors lose their sense of taste and desire more flavorful foods, and those with dementia often crave sweets. I know this to be true for my grandmother, and so I'm sensitive to this with her, but not so much to my Father who does not have dementia. He stopped drinking pop/soda when he came to live with us, but he has replaced it with sweet tea. I appreciate his effort in compromising, but it seems like a zero gain. In fact, for Father's Day last June, I bought him a FitBit, and at dinner in August, he announced that he was no longer wearing it. It seems that he'd gone to the doctor and discovered that he had gained 11 pounds. He stated that the only thing that changed in his life was wearing the FitBit, so it must be the cause….

It's interesting to see where we learn our lessons about one another come from, case in point: salsa. Or was it marinara sauce? That was the problem for me one night when I made myself nachos. Tortilla chips, shredded cheese, sliced avocado—with everything assembled, I opened the refrigerator to add the finishing touch;

I looked around and when I spotted it, I grabbed it: the salsa. It wasn't so hard to find—after all, it was there, clearly labeled in a Pace Salsa jar. I poured it on my nachos and dove in. Seconds later there was a full on revolution going on in my mouth. If my poor, disoriented and confused taste buds could talk, they would have said: "*What?!!! No way!!! Get this out of here.*" "This" was the marinara sauce that my mother had put in the salsa jar (without taking off the original salsa label.) That's the lesson I learned about living with other generations on this particular night. My generation throws the empty jars in the recycle bin, my mom's generation washes them out and reuses them. My kids' generation thinks differently about it all, too. When Adellina heard what had happened and offered to bring me something else to eat, she was shocked to learn that I had continued eating my nacho *con marinara*; she and her generation would have never done that, where I persevered in an act of hopeful optimism or stubborn defiance, Addie would have thrown it all out and been done with it.

I can't express how important it is to understand the intention behind the action when you have 4 generations in one household spanning several wars, incredible technological inventions, and the world becoming smaller and smaller. It's also critical to recognize the importance that upbringing plays when trying to comprehend another generation; what's been thought of as "normal" for their life experience probably isn't going to be "normal" for another generation. All of this generational living under the same roof has taught me to be tolerant of our generational differences, and while that might not always be easy, it's a lot easier when that understanding is also living under our roof!

Chapter 21

Big Brother Is Watching

Greg got a "NEST" thermostat that controls the temperature in the house. This means that he and I can access it from a phone app, and it also means that he and I can change the temperature wherever we may be, even if we are not at home.

How does this relate? Well, have you ever been around an older person and it's really warm, but they are really cold? That's because seniors have 70% less body fat than "20-somethings", and their body does not hold their core temperature like a younger adult's can. Seniors also tend to have slower metabolic rates, which means their bodies have a more difficult time generating heat. And if you throw in a medical condition such as heart disease, arthritis or diabetes, it's even more challenging for them to stay warm and comfortable.

This is such a huge deal; the normal core body temperature of 98.6 degrees can drop to what is considered hypothermia (below 95 degrees) if a senior has the home temperature set anywhere from 70-65 degrees in the winter. Factor in that older folks don't move around as much, and you can see how this is a legitimate issue.

Back to the NEST. Being able to adjust the temperature, remotely, if you feel the home was too hot or too cold - the idea sounded awesome!

However, the first couple months after getting the Nest, we were engaged in a battle over the temperature. Down it went, then up it went. Back down and then back up. Until Greg admitted he was lowering it when he was not at home. But guess who was at home? The older gens! Now Greg is not a mean guy, he just was noticing (from his cozy office) that it was hot at home. Maybe for his tastes and wallet.

A battle strategy would be needed to combat the war at hand:

Step 1. I explained the body fat issue to him.

Step 2. I explained the slower metabolism issue to him.

Step 3. I further "explained" that, unless he was there, he should not mess with our elders' heat storage issues "remotely."

Step 4. I explained to my parents that, if they could wear a sweater in the colder months, it would help balance out the temperature when we're all at home.

A truce was declared while the treaty was worked out between all parties. The conditions were as follows: the thermostat is now set at a warmer temperature, a balmy 72 in the winter, which is a bit more than the breezy 68-70 degrees that Greg and I think of as "normal." (And even though intellectually, Greg understands, I think it still bugs him.)

Today, Grandma uses a blanket when she's watching TV to keep comfortable, or puts on a cashmere sweater, which helps greatly.

Temperature is one of those funny things, you can't make others feel how you feel your temperature. It's one more example of how there's always the need for compromise - from all of us - if we're going to create balance in this 4Gen experiment.

Chapter 22

Failed Experiment

Our "lab" is full of experiments, some are brilliant successes, while others much less so. And so we often go back to the laboratory, re-think and tweak, holding out the hope for a better result the second time around (or third.) Sometimes it's not that the idea's failed, sometimes Grandma's condition has changed, and sometimes it's a little of both.

Recently, I had a brilliant idea (or so I thought). One that would eliminate the daily arguments my mom had with Grandma about taking her medications and vitamins. It was so simple, I couldn't believe I hadn't thought of it before: *stickers*. Grandma would place stickers on her Daytime calendar when she took her medicine. This way she'd know that my mom wasn't trying to "poison" her. And while she doesn't actually say it out loud, you can see it in her eyes, where there's a suspicious look whenever my mom hands her meds. Maybe that's why she sometimes hides them. If my mom leaves without actually seeing Grandma take her meds can often mean that later, Mom finds them hidden in a favorite spot: tucked in her chair or placed carefully in a napkin. Very deliberate actions that indicate they didn't just fall somewhere, they were very thoughtfully placed there.

The sticker idea seemed good on a few levels. First, she'd take the meds! Second, she'd be more independent. And third, we could change up the stickers seasonally to give her cues about the time of the year. Such a good idea! Except that it wasn't.

Like many ideas, it started out full of promise. I got the Day-Timer and got pretty rhinestones stickies, too. Mom explained the concept. Grandma thought it sounded great.

Day One: Grandma uses it and it goes well.

Day Two: Grandma and Mom argue. Grandma fussily asks: *"Why do I have to put this here?"* Mom calmly explains exactly why.

Day Three: No stickie! Mom, barely hanging onto calmness, explains, *"See, there's no stickie, so you didn't take your medicine."* Grandma responds: *"You just forgot to put the stickie on there, and I took my medicine."* I observe: how interesting it is that she can make a lie and have it be coherent, but she's not willing to play with the idea, of *"Maybe I didn't take it."*

Update One: We tweak it and make a change. Grandma has to *initial* the stickies. We'll see how she handles this. Will she deny it's her signature and accuse us of forging it? That's a possibility. If so, it'll be back to the laboratory for a new approach.

Update Two: Signature experiment shows promise on the first day, but ultimately fails by day three. And so back to the laboratory we go.

It's possible that I was just too late with this idea; two months ago I know she would have played along. But recently, Grandma's become more argumentative. Maybe it's the winter and not enough sun, maybe when the weather improves, she will too. But it's just as possible that she won't; she's shifted into a more disbelieving place, having more trouble with trust, and becoming a little bit paranoid.

CHAPTER 23

ROYAL FLUSH

In 2007 I had a chance to travel to Japan for an Entrepreneurs Organization (EO) conference. Typically, I don't bring my family on business trips, but EO is different; they support the whole entrepreneur and encourage spouses to come along - sometimes even kids. Since family trips Cini Style also means taking my parents along, I mentioned to everyone that, *"Japan would be an awesome trip for us all to go on."* Immediately, Grandma, then 86, piped up with an enthusiastic, *"I've always wanted to go to Japan!"* Frankly, I didn't even have her on the guest list, but it seemed like a once in a lifetime event that I couldn't possibly deny. And so the entire family, Grandma, my parents, my husband and kids (ages 10 and 13) flew off to Japan for what proved to be "an awesome trip," and all of us treasure the memories of it to this day.

Now what does this have to do with toilets?

Well, a lot, actually. While there, *every* toilet we experienced, even the public ones, had bidet seats on them that provided great comfort, greater cleanliness, and had a remarkably wide range of options. Among the options: a heated seat, a hidden wand that, at a touch of a button, would spray you off, and then, when you pressed another button your bum would be blow-dried. In simple terms... these toilets were frickin' awesome and we were frickin' impressed.

Arriving back home, I did some research and guess what Santa brought Greg (and me) for our master bathroom that Christmas?

A little background information. Not long before our Japan trip, we'd moved into a National Historic residence neighborhood. The kind that was gated and you have to be voted into. If you don't get my drift, think of it like this: most of the neighbors weren't baking pies and showing up to say: *"Howdy, folks, welcome to the neighborhood"*.

Now, back to Christmas season where I was waiting and waiting… for weeks…for the bidet. And nothing. I waited more and still nothing. Then I tracked the package and saw that a neighbor had signed for it. Great, now their first impression of me was the kook who came ringing their doorbell to ask if they'd signed for, and forgotten to give me, my toilet seat from Japan. And well, yes, that's exactly what their first impression was, because that's exactly what I did. And well yes, they had it, and well yes, it was as awkward as you can imagine. Not that it mattered, because when Christmas came and we installed the seat, Greg loved it.

And then the weirdness came. That's right, what you read above was *not* weird. Pretty soon, every single friend of my kids who would came over to the house would, when they had to use the bathroom, traipse upstairs, walk into my bedroom, and yep, you got it…beeline into my master bathroom and use our toilet. It didn't end there. Whenever we had a party, which we often did, we noticed the same exact phenomenon happening. Did I mention that we have 3 other common bathrooms? Yet everyone felt completely comfortable entering our master bedroom to get to the master bathroom toilet. When I happened to mention this to my friends, I was surprised at their reaction: they knew all about it. Turns out the "Cini toilet" was the talk of the town.

A few years later, we decided to sell that home and begin our new multi-generational lifestyle. And while we didn't know a lot of the details regarding what was going to happen, we did know one thing: the 4Gen Experiment would include many bidet toilet seats that could wash and blow-dry. But I have to admit, it was not just because I loved my bidet toilet seat and all its neighborhood acclaim; there was a different reason, too, which was lying in the answer to this question: *How can I avoid having to wipe my parents bum if they have surgery or something happens to them?* It's not as strangely hypothetical as it might sound. When my mother-in-law had surgery, my sisters-in-law had to help her go to the bathroom, which also meant helping clean her - embarrassing for my mother-in-law, and tough on Greg's sisters. So when I thought about that *not* having that happen to me, my next thought was about the bidet toilet seat. And at $350.00 per toilet, it seemed like a small price to pay for *their* dignity and *my* sanity. And not just mine, but for my mom's too, who was to be the primary caregiver for my grandmother.

After she settled in from the big move, and our Social Experiment was up and running, one day I asked Grandma if my mother had shown her how it worked and how she liked it. I don't know why, but I was shocked to hear that she loved it! I didn't remember that Grandma, 93 at the time, was completely able to understand it and use it all by herself. I'd forgotten that she was no virgin to technology, and that she'd seen more changes in technology than any of us; the development of new-fangled things such as: the car, indoor plumbing, radio, TV, phone, cell phone, electricity and the Internet. When you think about it like that, really, would a toilet that could wash and dry you be such a big deal?

And she had a reason that she liked it, too: it let her take care of herself, without being a burden on my mother. With her shower, she needed help, but the toilet seat allowed her to (basically) take a "sitz bath." My age group doesn't quite get this concept, but for folks her age, this is what they grew up doing; water was either collected in a rain barrel, or from a well, or sometimes, if you had the luxury, the city got water to you. Regardless, water was not something you could waste. Women would often use a sitz bath for "personal hygiene", so this wildly new contraption (in our minds) was in a sense, incredibly familiar to her.

The bidet has fans and other options, too. I remember, with absolute clarity (and delight) the first time my father, a combination of Robert De Niro and Archie Bunker, used his bidet seat. Since he did not *exactly* read the manual from cover to cover, he went in and a moment later came out screaming that he had a *"G.D. tornado up his A."* After some quick coaching on the settings, he turned his way down from "high" and very soon he, too, came to love the bidet toilet seat. Grandma did not have the same model as my father. We were testing out different manufacturers on each toilet to see our likes and dislikes. I can honestly say, I am not sure why the setting *"Vortex"* should ever be on one of these bidet toilet seats, but my father was the lucky one to try it out.

My daughter's graduation party speaks to the bidet's widespread appeal. Since we had several hundred guests, we rented port-a-potties. Guess what happened *anyway*? I had parents coming to me and asking if they could use the toilets *inside,* because they had heard so much about them. It's a weird conversation to be sure, but it also goes to show how amazing they are.

Since our Social Experiment started, we have finally been able to convince some of our senior living clients to put them in their apartments! The lesson here is that with a small dollar investment you can increase the dignity and independence of your loved one and reduce your burden. The positives end up being for everyone, which is a huge win-win.

CHAPTER 24

SAFETY FIRST

My mom and dad have been taking Grandma out for car rides, almost like what Greg and I did when our kids were little and we wanted to settle them down when they were agitated.

However, maneuvering a 137-pound elderly woman with stiff joints, and achy bones, is not easy, definitely not as easy as with a 25 or 30 pound kid. Still, as tough as it is on them, my mom and dad do it because it's great for Grandma. The drive gives her a change in her daily visual perspective and she gets to see new things. Knowing she's going out also forces her to make a greater effort and put on a prettier outfit. Plus, Grandma's still able to "perform" when she's out in public and behave like a "good adult" behaves, which is good for her to do on a regular basis. Even though just getting her in and out of the car could take at least ten minutes, not only are my mom and dad doing this constantly, but they do it with a lot of love and care.

That's why it was so surprising when one day, while their old car was moving, Grandma opened the door.

Dad stepped sharply on the brakes, got out from behind the wheel and closed her door. And having done that, he started moving again.

A few minutes later she managed to open that door up again. And again Dad stepped on the brakes, again he got out and again he locked her in, but this time he manually found the child lock inside her door and solved the issue. Then he went back to his seat and started the car. And though it didn't happen, my mom went to a worst-case scenario… *"Oh my god, what if Grandma fell out??!!"* She worries like that. And then, for good measure, she also worries about a lot of things *like that*. Beyond that, she also worries about it from the standpoint of being Grandma's caretaker and wondering what others would say if it did happen. Would they accuse her of not watching out for Grandma? What would everyone think?

That's the problem when you're a caretaker - no one's willing to make the sacrifice or actually provide the care, but they're always willing to advise you about the care you're giving, and they're always ready to tell you what you're doing wrong.

My mom and I talk about this a lot. I tell her what a great job she's doing, and how careful and loving she is with Grandma. And it's the absolute truth. What else is true is that she does so much and gets so little appreciation or praise. I guess that lack of support now makes her a true and official caregiver, because no caregiver I know gets the positive acknowledgements they really deserve.

Chapter 25

Always a Lady

Once a week, Grandma goes to the Holiday Beauty Salon. And for as long as she can, this weekly event is going to be on her calendar. It's more than just looking better when she leaves than when she walked in, though that matters an awful lot to her since Grandma is a staunch believer in the idea that "it's more important to look good than it is to feel good." But this visiting the salon is important for its social value, too. It's that weekly check-in, that weekly connection; it's someone asking her *"How're the great grandchildren?", "How're the grandchildren?", "How're the children?"*

Going to the salon is something for Grandma to just simply delight in. And I've seen what happens when she's there: she relaxes deeply, and enjoy herself immensely. I think other things are going on too, things that bring the relaxation and the enjoyment. Here, in the beauty salon, Grandma relishes being touched in a loving and caring way. She gets warm caresses on her shoulders and her neck. If she has her nails done, her hands are held and rubbed. And always, without fail, she gets her head massaged, which not only feels great, it also helps get her blood flowing up there. It's not like we don't hug and kiss Grandma. As I've said before, we're an Italian family and that's a big part of our culture. But in her salon, she gets touched more, and in such a very positive, non-medical way, and that's really great for her spirit.

But maybe even more than anything else, the reason we'll keep this on her calendar as long as possible, is that her outlook on life improves simply by being in the salon, and I have to think that's because of the sense of community she's created at Holiday. As her loved ones and friends have died, Grandma's circle has become smaller and smaller, and so expanding her circle through other relationships is critical, as is being able to share the ups and downs of life with them, too. My 94-year old grandmother knows everything about her salon friends' families and extended families, and they know a lot about hers, too.

And while sometimes that might scare me a little bit, most times I just think it's a very wonderful thing. And let's not forget the impact on how feeling pretty and "remade" gets her ready to address the world again. Shallow? Not for Grandma, for Grandma it's just the truth.

CHAPTER 26

THE BEES

We live in the city on a decent sized lot with lots of trees. We also have a lake house, or "cabin", which my husband Greg considers, "camping." This says more about Greg than about the house, because really, it's not camping at all as our lake cabin has everything our city house does *and* with a beautiful lake view. So imagine my surprise when my city guy, a guy who loves staying at the nicest hotels, hates camping, and never gardens, announced, after watching an episode of Shark Tank, that we were getting bees!

I looked at him and thought, *"This guy's going to raise bees?"* Which led me to ask him, *"Why?"* His answer made so much sense and again, it said more about Greg than about bees. He felt it came down to how much joy the bird feeders gave my grandmother and mother, and so he thought the bees could be one more activity for them to enjoy. As well as all of us benefitting from the honey, and helping the world in the process.

How does Shark Tank play into all of this? Apparently, in an episode Greg saw, a person pitched a beehive that let people get the honey out without disturbing the bees. In this system, the honey flows out from a spigot. Greg bought one before they had even started producing them.

Today, Grandma has full view of the beehive on her circuit to the family room. Every Saturday, after Greg comes back from his four-hour weekly bee class, he and my mom spend hours (literally) talking about how awesome bees are. And the bees? Well, they've already started to produce honey, which is not at all surprising if you see the way they zoom in and out of the hive like a squadron of World War II bombardiers.

I have to admit that what I've learned about them so far is not only interesting, but it's also inspiring. They each have a purpose in the hive and they work together to make sure the hive is successful. They sacrifice for each other, but that's their strength. As I said earlier in the book, I think our social experiment is similar to the beehive, and had we not started down this road, there would be so many things I would have missed or we would have not learned about each other and the world.

CHAPTER 27

TWO KINDS OF GIVING

There are two kinds of giving that Grandma needs: physical and emotional. The interesting thing about these two kinds of needs is that the physical ones tend to be more valued by the person performing them, while the more emotional needs are more valued by the person with Alzheimer's/Dementia. And our family is split on who does which.

My mom (primarily) and my 18-year-old daughter, Adellina, are more part of Grandma's "physical" giving team. They help bathe her, clothe her, take her to her appointments, and their efforts are pretty tangible. It's clear when Grandma's eaten, clear if she goes outside, clear if her meds are taken. They feel good about getting Grandma to do these things, even if their efforts are the ones that receive more pushback from Grandma, especially on the days that she's not as lucid, and is more argumentative and agitated.

Then there's Jake, my 21-old-son. When it comes to Grandma, he's definitely an "emotional" giver, and she loves it and loves him for it. He'll often do things like play the piano for her, watch a sports game with her, or tell her about his soccer. None of which require that Grandma *do* anything, she just has to *"be"* -- whoever she is right then.

Grandma doesn't simply respond to this emotional kind of attention, she absolutely lights up and becomes herself when she gets it. But the giver of this kind of attention can often get the short end of the stick in the appreciation department; emotional giving is almost intuitive, and so, unfortunately, it's often less valued. But it shouldn't be. Both hold equal weight in Grandma's life, and she needs both to thrive.

Knowing which kind of "giver" you are is important; it helps you go into situations with your eyes open and your expectations clear. However, not just yours, but also all the other people who are involved with the care and support as well. And maybe most of all, the love of the person who's the object of all your attentions.

Chapter 28

Grandma as Weather Girl

Grandma's our weather girl. From her primary lookout spot in the Dining Room, which also serves as her primary bird watching spot, she takes in the changes of weather - something she's always liked doing. With that in mind, Greg hit on the idea of putting up a thermometer right outside her favorite viewing spot.

These days we're not so sure what Grandma's taking in and what she isn't. So it was surprising, and also incredibly gratifying, when 15 minutes after Greg put it up, she came and found us and told us it was, "Perfect!"

Grandma doesn't only use it for weather reporting, though, she also uses it to assess risks for herself. If my mother wants to take Grandma out for a meal, Grandma might look at the thermometer and say, "No, not today, it's not worth the trouble; it's too cold and too hard to bundle up."

We didn't know at the time, but this thermometer has also become a way for Grandma to engage with all of us. She'll read the thermometer and then tell us how cold it'll be and to put on a hat, and take a scarf. In the summer, we'll learn that we're over-dressed.

What's so gratifying to us is that we get to catch glimpses of the Grandma we remember, the one who's really living her life. Who would have thought that a simple thermometer could give us all this happy peek into her again?

Chapter 29

The Rise of a Sneaky Grandma

Grandma's sneaky when we're not watching. Actually, she's pretty sneaky when we're watching, too, and I'm starting to see it a little more and more, especially when it comes to situations that involve, guess who? My mother, of course.

We have a rescue dog, Callie, who loves us all, but perhaps loves Grandma best. Callie's no dummy, she knows that Grandma tends to let her out the most, and pays attention to her the most, too. But even more than that, Grandma's the one who feeds Callie the most cookies. And that's where the issue with my mom started, and continues. Mom asked her not to feed Callie too many cookies, but as soon as she turns her back, or leaves the room, I'll catch Grandma giving Callie a cookie. And with a sneaky wink and a determined nod, she'll tells me, *"She can't tell me what to do."*

I understand that this her way of just trying to maintain her adult/mother status a little longer, and in any way she can. So what I do is try to get her into a conversation. Actually, I see it as a rare (and sadly, getting rarer) treat. In these situations, she's full of life, she's got a twinkle in her eye, she's 110% there and I want to have that moment with her, and so I'm all in. Plus, the senior living training

I've had often focused on the concept of *"not arguing."* We were told to ask ourselves, *"Is it really going to hurt the situation"* And if not, then *"play along,"* because it's her reality, it's her perspective.

If I do think it's something that's going to hurt her, it's a very different thing. And if that starts happening more and with greater frequency, we will probably have to consider a different situation for Grandma. Our goal is for her to stay in her home/our home with her loved ones as long as possible, but we also know that at some point, the best thing might be to put her in an environment where she'll be cared for by professionally trained people, people who are respectful, non-emotional and who won't get upset when they're asked for the same thing seven times. But until that day comes, I'll enjoy playing along with Grandma as long as I can. And make sure my pet insurance is up to date!

CHAPTER 30

WHO RESCUED WHO?

We adopted Callie (the rescue dog) several years ago. She looks a lot like Benji, if you remember the movies. It's not clear whether Callie was rescued or if Callie has done the rescuing. She provides daily comfort, security and activity to my grandmother, mother and father.

She keeps Grandma on her toes by "asking" to go outside and then come back in several times a day, this is only interrupted by begging to be petted, watching the comings and goings of the neighborhood on the front porch and then eating.

Callie is my mother's alarm clock, as twice a day you can set your watch to when she is supposed to eat and if she has to wait, she becomes obnoxious with her actually trying to "talk" to my mother in dog speak vs. barking.

She provides so much love, touch, and comfort it's amazing, well for most of the family. My father and Callie have a love/hate relationship. She nudges him every morning to pet her, swims with him and they go on walks, but at night when he gets up from his recliner and moves to the bed, all heck breaks loose. You would have thought an intruder just tried to break in. She raises a fit barking "mean" at him. And so this, their "dance," goes until he is in bed.

We don't know why it happens; it's just more noises that come out of my parent's suite that I try not to understand.

By now, we've known each other long enough that you understand our family has a bit of a sense of humor and how important it is to an experiment of this kind. It's recently been extremely hot, so my father and Callie were swimming in the pool. Apparently, he asked her if she wanted to race (Mom, Dad and Grandma all believe Callie understands their every word and I am inclined to believe them). Rising to his challenge, Callie takes off for the end of the pool and she gets almost to the end and turns around on her way to the finish line. Just as this happens, my father's head surfaces from the swim and he sees her beating him, and so he yells out to anyone that will listen, "*You didn't tap! I WIN!*" Yes you read that right… I asked him if he was serious, and he said of course, and he meant it.

Even with Callie turning into a vicious attack dog when my father leaves his recliner, she always would protect him and all of us to the death. When he had both his knees replaced, she would not leave his side, she knew her job was now to be the alpha and let him heal. When Grandma's not well, she does the same, even if we think Grandma's okay. Animals have a sixth sense that can tell when we need protecting or nurturing. To this day, we think she rescued all of us and continues to provide comfort, safety and love for the price of a square meal or cookie.

Chapter 31

Not In My House

A little background is necessary to understand the following story. While there are five siblings in my family, I have always taken the stance that we were conceived by immaculate conception. Sex was not something that was discussed in our family. I remember reading Judy Bloom to get all of my information regarding the subject, and was quite happy that my parents never desired to have the "talk". One miraculous day, a book just appeared in my bedroom. I remember reading it in my closet, by flashlight. I never mentioned the book to anyone, and no one mentioned it to me.

As we became adults and had kids of our own, my parents would make jokes about their sex life to make us uncomfortable. You know the kind: *"Honey did you pick up the Viagra?"* Seeing me cringe, they'd become like sharks that just got the scent of blood, and then they'd really pour it on to make me even more uncomfortable. At which time, I would respond as any typical adult child would with my fingers in my ears and making sounds to drown them out until they stopped torturing me.

One night, shortly after my parents moved in with us, I heard a noise unlike any that I heard before. It was a moaning. A very expressive and loud moaning. An almost desperate moaning. It was obviously coming from my mother, and she was saying *"Oh... Johnny....Oh......Johnny..................."*

I nearly lost my mind. And then I thought,*"Oh no, not in my house! This is a NO GO. I love you and all, but I can't handle this."*

So instead of ignoring all the moaning and all of the calling out of my father's name, I sat straight up in bed, and decided to take charge. I would break up this nonsense! I would inform my parents this behavior would have to stop! And furthermore, it would not happen again! (Unless they wanted me in the looney bin, which would result in them having to find living accommodations elsewhere, because I would be unfit to work!)

I charged through 5 doors to make it into their suite. And then I busted open their door. Only to find...my father on his knees rubbing my mother's calf and trying to get rid of her leg cramp. I can't tell you how relieved I was that this was not what I was expecting. The images running through my mind were getting more and more outrageous by the minute, and truth be told, if I had seen them in the "act,"

I would have caused myself way more damage. I don't think I could ever "unsee" what I thought I was going to see. But the drive to stop the action was greater than understanding the possible consequences.

I told them what I thought was going on and we all had a great laugh. Then I went downstairs, grabbed her a banana, and with all of its much needed potassium, soon the cramp was over. They had a lot of fun telling the story for the next couple of weeks.

Living with 4-Generations has lots of challenges but also lots of fun. You never know what to expect or how you will react. I certainly never thought I would have reacted in this way, but I did. Our greatest joys and bonds have been when we have been able to laugh at a situation.

CHAPTER 32

THE LUNCH BUNCH

Every Thursday, of every week, my mom takes Grandma out to lunch.

And they're not the only ones.

My mom's good friends bring their Mom's, too. And their rendezvous spot of choice is Scotty's Cafe, a local diner in town. These original twelve women are affectionately known as, no, not The Dirty Dozen, and not The Apostles, but rather they go by The Lunch Bunch, and they've been going six years!

When the Grandkids, or Great-Grandkids, are in town, on break from college, grad school or whatever they're pursuing, the pilgrimage is made to Scotty's. They've come from all parts of the country and the world, and they share their adventures like war veterans or pirates at dock. The Lunch Bunch can follow every detail, as they have been keeping track of all of their moves. These kids really connect with, and stay connected to, these older generations. They don't see them as a "throw away" group of people, and they're not just someone they know who gives them money in an envelope; these are people they sit with, talk to and enjoy spending their time with.

But it doesn't stop there. There's a ripple effect that can be seen across the world connecting a multitude of generations, faiths and cultures. To explain a little further, at lunch there can be multiple sets of 4 Generations and they're from Christian and Jewish backgrounds. The Grandkids are discovering themselves and a lot of them are traveling while doing so. Adellina (my daughter) lives in Rome, Italy studying archeology. One of her best friends, Selin, is from Istanbul. When Jordy, one of the other Lunch Bunch Grandkids (Gerta's Grandson, and my son Jacob's best friend) was studying abroad in Prague, and Addie was in Rome, the Grandmas got together planning and plotting for them to be able to see each other. It was finally all set, through Viber, Snap Chat, Facebook etc. (Yes, the Grandmas use technology). The day Jordy and Adellina were to meet in Rome, Selin happened to be there, too, visiting Addie, and Selin asked, "*Is that Gerta's grandson?*" Addie was amazed, but then realized how much she talks about her Grandma and Great Grandma's Lunch Bunch and how she relays all the fun stories to her friends. These women range from 47 to 94 and have figured out a way to connect each week with not only each other, but halfway around the world.

When they go to leave, Scotty announces to the entire restaurant "*Attention everyone! The retired cast of the Radio City Music Hall Rockettes are about to leave the building.*" Everyone gets a big kick out of it, no pun intended.

For Grandma, all of these things - going out every week to the Hair Salon, and meeting up with The Lunch Bunch, serve as a barometer for my understanding of where she is in her health. I know if she doesn't want to go to the Salon, or to The Lunch Bunch, something is up, and I'll try to check in and try even harder to understand what's happening. But equally important is that it gives Grandma a way to stay engaged in her life, and to interact with people who love to see her and let her know how important she is to them, and how much they love her. What more is there to life than that?

CHAPTER 33

OUR BOARDERS

My Italian grandmother "Della" would have these incredible Sunday dinners with tons of people that I thought were all family. As I grew older, I asked how is "so and so" related? Then I found out that some of them were borders; this was especially the case when times were tough. One gentleman, "Mix Paulmier," was apparently only supposed to stay for a couple days, but ended up living with my grandparents for eight years. While we've had various boarders of our own, all have been family...*until now.*

This all started when my son Jake left for college and I converted his bedroom to a guest room, and then I left for a trip. When I returned, I found that the guest bedroom had "boarders" staying in there, six to be exact. One was black, one was white, one was mixed and three were yellow. You're probably thinking the room was enormous, but it isn't. The "boarders" were baby chicks.

To back up, a plan had been hatched between my husband, Greg, my mother and my Daughter Adellina. (Notice who was left out of the planning? Right, me.) Now remember that Greg was also the mastermind behind the idea of providing a place for bees to live happily at the 4-Generation home, and in truth that has worked out pretty well, so his suggestion that we should now raise chickens, might not really be a big surprise. Well, they all agreed and then he sprung the idea on me. My initial shock, and possible resistance, was dealt with via a bribe: they'd get their chickens and I'd get my bocce court (which I'd always wanted). But while I did agree, little did I know they would become borders in my house for TWO MONTHS!

And oh, by the way, Della had these kinds of "borders" too, 700 hundred to be exact! It's funny what you learn in these kinds of experiments: the stories that keep coming from my parents… that I'd never heard before…have been awesome! My father relayed that not only had his mother raised 700 chickens, but also that he had a funny incident of his own with chickens. When my mother added in that it almost caused a divorce, we all settled in to listen.

Apparently, before I was born, my mother saw an ad in the newspaper: *"Chickens for sale for 20 cents per pound in Amish Country."* This was incredible, and times were tight… so she bought several pounds and let my father know the address where he was supposed to pick them up.

His car wouldn't hold all the boxes, but that wasn't a problem. He ended up working that Saturday and decided to borrow a co-worker's station wagon (that she had borrowed from her brother.) When lunchtime rolled around, Dad rolled out to pick them up.

Imagine his surprise when he arrived and the man behind the ad brought out live chickens! Dad argued that, *"They were supposed to be dead not alive,"* but ultimately, he lost the battle and went back to work, arriving just when his lunch break ended. A little later, someone found my Dad and told him there was an issue and he needed to come to the parking lot right away. Dad gets there to find the chickens have gotten out of their cage and are all over the inside of the station wagon. There's even one sitting on the steering wheel doing his business!

He spent hours cleaning out the borrowed car of all the feathers and droppings. He had to pay a butcher to kill, and then clean the chickens. And for many years, Dad was the brunt of jokes at work.

We all laughed so hard we cried, and Mom and Dad loved retelling what would have been a lost story.

In case you have never raised chickens... chicks are cute as buttons to start. Then they morph into ugly teenagers, and suddenly they look half cute and half like a raptor from Jurassic Park. My daughter named them after Disney princesses: Belle, Rapunzel, Jasmine, Snow, Cruella (not a princess but still Disney) and Pocahontas.

Our "boarders" all learned their names and would hop out of the brooder box as soon as my daughter Adellina entered the room. They would let us pet them and even climb on us. But chickens do an odd thing; when they want to look at you they turn their heads sideways so their eye is closer to you. This, accompanied by their dinosaur feet, can scare you a bit if you're not comfortable with animals.

My grandmother, Mother, Greg and I all interacted with them daily, so did Adellina when she was at home from college; we all found them endearing, not my 21-year-old son Jacob. He admitted to the family that he went into his bedroom (now overtaken by the "borders") and bent down to get a charger. In a matter of moments, Jake was cornered by all 6 Disney princesses. Thinking they were a lot more like raptors, he froze in his tracks. Too scared to move for fear of attack, Jake whimpered out a sad "Mammal.......Mammal" hoping his Grandma would come to his rescue. They were eyeing him, heads turned, and beaks ready to strike. Finally, after 20 minutes of not moving a muscle, he was able to escape. At the dinner table this story was relayed and we laughed until we cried.

I bring these stories up, because they wouldn't have happened, or been relayed, had we not decided to raise chickens. They connected us to our past and present and gave us memories that we will all cherish for the rest of our lives (okay, maybe not Jake.) Laughter is one of the greatest connections we have with each other, it feeds the soul.

Field Note Update:

The "boarders" moved out. To the coop. And then came the nest camera. Now Adellina can check in on her Princesses all the way from Rome. Yes, she can also stay connected to conversation with the family, just like she could when she was home from college. Jacob has no interest in the nest camera.

CHAPTER 34

"GOD, WHY NOT HER?"

On August 24th 2014 my mother, father and 93-year-old grandmother moved in with our family. One week later, on August 31st 2014, at around 6 am in the morning, I heard a blood-curdling scream from my mother. My immediate thought was that my father had died.

I ran into their room to see my father talking on the phone and my mom tell me my 19-year-old nephew, Matt, was dead. He was killed in the middle of the night in a car accident.

In a moment, the unimaginable happened and my life, my family's, and all those who knew and loved Matt would never be the same. We were forever changed - from our thoughts and interactions, down to and into, our dreams.

While you might think this is about regrets, it's not. It's also not about feeling sorry for me or my family. It's just about life and how to get the most out of every drop, every breath, every connection and to be able to laugh when the unimaginable happens, sometimes through the tears.

To provide some context, my family had been blessed up to this point with very little death, and those we had experienced were people who lived long full lives 90, 92, 99 & 100 years old. Jokes would often be made as to who would put the pillow over Grandpa's head (poor taste, I know), because he just seemed to keep on going like the Eveready Bunny! Funerals were a family reunion, a place to tell great stories of fun and adventure and to honor, while celebrating the life that was no longer with us.

While I cannot get over the loss of Matt, I have no regrets. How could I possibly say this? It is because I was brought up to SHOW UP. You could never walk into a family gathering without feeling like you were on the witness stand, getting questioned on where and what you were doing. My relatives were interested, very interested. Over the years, we started a few cherished traditions at Thanksgiving and Christmas that required us to SHOW UP.

Years ago, my mother started a family Thanksgiving tradition of writing, on a linen tablecloth, what we were thankful for. We'd all put a date on it, and then we we'd all add to it year after year.

Christmas, we would all sing Christmas carols as kids, and then Santa would come. At this point, his "elf" would pull out a present and start reading from the "book." This book was special…it was *old*. It had things about my father, my kids, and me in it. But the most interesting thing about this book was that it told of, not only what you had done that was good over the year, but also what was bad and you needed to work on! For instance, *"Johnny was very good helping around the house, but needs to work on his math."* The crowd would cheer, "yay" for the good, and moan, "ohhh" for the bad. You learned very early you had to SHOW UP because the family cared and you were accountable to them all to be your best you. There was no parental cover-ups, and never an "everyone gets a trophy" philosophy in my family.

I carried this on in my own way by making my children, nieces and nephews SHOW UP from the time they were small and we were on vacations or at our lake cottage or the ocean. They would roll their eyes and complain a bit, but secretly they loved it.

SHOWING UP meant telling me, and each other, all of their dreams and challenges. They had to share these and were told they were loved and valued, but they also had to do this with their siblings, cousins and friends. They had to teach how to show up to those younger.

This ultimately resulted in Matt, my son Jacob, and I starting a company for extreme sports clothing called "*Intersect,*" when they were 15. We would discuss their dreams and challenges and we would work them out. Matt would always show up and talk me through his latest dream, and then do the work associated with figuring it out. When he was 18, he spent 3 days with me doing this!

It wasn't just Matt that I did this with, of my best memories is of my kids, all of the nieces and nephews and their friends, when I was able to hear what they were excited about, their dreams and see them move forward and even help others.

There's something incredibly intimate when someone lets you into their dreams and fears and when you are able to help them, there's no greater high, or greater love.

So you see there are no regrets. What I learned from Matt's death was that because we required Showing Up, we left nothing unsaid.

I did have issues with God during all of this, and learned that coping with tragedy is more complex than I had imagined. As horrible as this may sound, I was mad at God. I believe that God gave us breath to do wonderful things for the world, and if we are not adding value to the world, and instead, we're just waiting to die, then we should leave. But now Matt's life was gone and others were taking up space? God, why not her? There I said it. And now I'll add to it. Why, God, would you take this incredible life - that was just starting to bloom - and cut it down vs. taking my grandmother at 93, with dementia, who has actively said she is fine with dying. Hopefully by now you realize I deeply love my grandmother and honor and respect her, but she has lived a full life and now lives somewhere in-between life and death, not knowing reality and struggling day in day out. So at this point I was having trouble making sense of it all.

Through this, I have learned that coping with tragedy and death is something that, as we age, we have to experience more and more. What used to seem to be the random relative dying, who you barely knew, became your grandparents, older close relatives and sadly even parents, and the unthinkable, a child.

In our 4-Gen Experiment, it seems that my parents and grandmother seem to be talking about someone they knew or loved passing monthly. Living together exposes the kids, and Greg, and me to this constant barrage of who is sick and dying or has just passed. I don't mean to be insensitive, but it's a little like living in a war zone. Few of my friends, and none of my kids' friends are in the midst of this daily depressing discussion; they live void of this kind of news, except for family holidays or calls. And it wears on you, like watching the news of horrible things happening all around the world 24/7. You either want to avoid it altogether and stick you head in the sand, or you become overly sensitive as I had, when I found myself asking them to stop talking about everyone's hip replacements, cancer, heart issues, dementia, cataracts and so on.

Finding a balance to this generational issue comes down to a mutual understanding. For my parents and grandmother, they need to be able to express their heartache and grief. Spouses, sisters, brothers, cousins and friends are dying all around them. It's like they're living their lives in Agatha Christie's book, *And Then There Were None*. On the flip side, every conversation with my mother should not start off by telling me what's on the family news wire of who's sick, dying or just passed. When you hear this negative news (while it's important), it makes you want to avoid having conversations with them altogether.

What I have found that works is an open, honest conversation about this. It's critical for everyone to be sensitive to the situation, what should be shared, how to do it in order to avoid disconnection or sarcasm.

While all of this talk of tragedy is a bit depressing, it was a godsend having my parents and grandmother in our house when Matt passed. We were able to support them and they us. We did not have to think twice as to which houses to go to for all the needed gatherings for Matt. It became a no brainer to host Thanksgiving and Christmas with my Parents and Grandma living with us.

Thanksgiving was a couple months after his funeral, and we all gathered around the table and held hands and said what we were thankful for, just like we had in prior years. We were blessed to be able to read Matt's writing on the tablecloth, as well as others who had passed, and carry their love with and in us. We all committed to *"overuse I love you"* (as Matt was a fan of saying) and supported each other through the painful loss and wonderful memories.

I leave you with these simple ideas to get through the challenges of loss: *"Overuse I love you,"* walk in each other's shoes, communicate and support each other with honest conversation and lastly, it's okay to think thoughts you might be embarrassed about. *"Why not her"*... helped me to work through the process of loss and realize I had no regrets.

CHAPTER 35

SAYING GOODBYE

Every time the kids leave I say, *"Go kiss your Great Grandma, she might not be here the next time you come back."*

This is not me being morbid. It's me asking them to make a mental note that reminds them to take a pause. It's me saying, *"Your life is moving so fast, slow it down and have a moment that's about her, because her life is not going fast, hers is going slower and slower."*

What this is about, and what so much of our "experiment" is about, is meeting someone, and most especially, Grandma, where she is. So slow down, say goodbye, take a moment. They love her dearly and appreciate the reminder…most of the time.

As you just read in the previous chapter, we know this lessen more deeply than most families, because of my 19-year-old nephew's recent passing. Matt was fond of posting his thoughts on Instagram and Facebook, and one of his quotes we all cherish and try to live by is *"Over use I LOVE YOU."* It's simple, yet profound, and worth repeating.

CHAPTER 36

UNTIL WE MEET

I fly a lot; by a lot, I mean 3-6 flights a week, typically all over the country. You become pretty good at starting conversations with folks waiting for the plane, or on a flight. Nine times out of ten the conversation works around to asking me what I do for a living, and why I am traveling to so and so city.

As I mention that I design for Alzheimer's and Dementia, I see them light up. It was weird at first; it would be like someone getting excited to hear you design cancer clinics! But what I realized is that there's so little information out there for those who have loved ones suffering from Alzheimer's and Dementia, and even less information related to design tips and tricks.

I always try to give them ideas of how they can manage the situation better, as well as concepts I've researched and implemented in our Hive.

If we don't end up meeting in the airport someday, here are some helpful hints until we do.

1. Don't argue with a person with Alzheimer's or Dementia.
2. Play along when they call you by the wrong name.
3. Involve them in daily chores such as folding clothes or setting the table.

4. Make sure they get plenty of sunshine.

5. Don't let them sleep too much during the day.

6. Make sure their choices are limited– this relates to everything, the less choice the less confusion.

7. Change the plate they eat on to a red one, or something that contrasts with the food, so it is easier to see.

8. Make sure they drink plenty of water.

9. Use juice vs. water for taking pills – it makes the pills easier to swallow.

10. Have a night light by the toilet.

11. Remove clutter and cords from the floor.

12. Use coconut oil on their food (Brain Octane from Bullet Proof Coffee is what we use.)

13. Make them walk or exercise; it gets the blood flowing and helps the brain have more oxygen.

14. Make sure decorations around the house are appropriately seasonal I.E. Christmas when it's Christmas, Spring flowers for Spring, Fall for Fall, etc.

15. Make sure that lights are bright enough, and if possible, get a light that mimics sunshine—it helps regulate their circadian cycle, which helps them sleep better.

16. Program the TV like you would for a child with a few channels they like, vs. 255 channels to choose from.

17. Add a camera system so you don't become a prisoner, or feel like you have to check on them in person, constantly, to make sure they are okay.

18. Make sure they have an event weekly, preferably two, that gets them out of the house. It could be a trip to the beauty salon or barber, or out to lunch with friends.

19. Meet them where they are, remember they are doing the best they can, and they can get quite frustrated with their inability to remember.

20. If they seem to go back in time to when they were younger, try giving them items that help them reminisce. If they

rewound the clock and just became 19 and are newly married, give them a basket with wedding photos, some lace, etc. for discussion and remembering.

21. Listen to their stories and remember that not too long from now, you may not be able to.

I hope that we do meet one day, but until we do, my wish is that your life and theirs is better from our paths crossing, if only in written form.

BONUS

Yoga – By Lori Allen

As we age, our options for exercise become more and more limited. This is unfortunate, because if there was ever a time for us to remain physically fit, it is in our senior years. After all, there are a host of ailments and diseases that come about because of inactivity, or are at least made much worse by it. Yoga for seniors is a no brainer the word itself literally means "to join" or "to unite". Bringing together mind, body and spirit.

The physical effects of yoga are well documented: the exercise helps individuals achieve greater flexibility, lubricate joints and tendons, improves respiratory health, balance and tone muscles. Likewise, the psychological effects are tremendous as well: yoga fosters a sense of calm wellbeing and promotes community bringing people together lessening their feelings of isolation.

A typical senior gets weaker and tighter as they sit for long hours. This can result in muscle shortening and loss of range in motion. They can also develop osteoporosis, and their balance becomes worse. This leads not only to greater deterioration of their bones and muscles, but it can lead to accidents as well. Yoga can help to counteract these problems. It can help to stretch a senior's muscles, preventing that tightness and shortening. It can help maintain healthy bones, and best of all, it can help seniors maintain a sense of balance and that's just the physical benefits. Yoga is empowering and as a senior ages they feel a loss of control in their lives. Yoga can help bring that control back creating a sense of empowerment, overall higher quality of life, better emotional health, and even an increase in socialization.

They best news is yoga is for every "body" whether performed in a chair, lying on the ground or standing, yoga does not discriminate.

"I am powerful. I am healthy. I am strong. I feel safe, I am loved. Namaste"

Nutrition

o   Bullet Proof Coffee – Brain Octane and Unfair Advantage

Blog

o   Check out blog for updates – www.lisamcini.com

Products

- **Best Living Tech** – for items mentioned in the book for purchase check out www.bestlivingtech.com
- I good friend of mine has a wonderful company that helps to ease the burden of having everything in one spot easy to find for family members. Jon asked me "If something happened to you today, would your family know where to find your advance directives or even know your final wishes? What about your banking information, insurance policies, Will or even how to access your credit card information or social media accounts?" I was embarrassed to say no….. but now I do and you can also. Jon has graciously given all our readers a discount code to you. This will provide 50% of the 1st year subscription of $79. Just go to www.mylifeandwishes.com and enter the code: **LISAMCINI50**

Acknowledgements

Matthew John Miller – "Little Matt" you lived and loved to the fullest, I will strive to Overuse I LOVE YOU. 548 Forever

The Lunch Bunch: Libby Miller, Gerline Lilly, Madeline Fields, Gerda Almashanu, June Creith, Patty Lorms, Margot Marx, Peggy Mc Cann, Donna Fulford, Lorie Onda, Betty Powell, Mary Kravitz, Kim Yee, Joanne Bristol, Ginny Olson, Marian Dash, Dorothy Vish, Joni Dragin &Kay Fothergill

The Lunch Bunch kids – Addie and Jacob Cini, Jordy Hoffman, Aaron Sugarman, Scott Sugarman, Noah Hoffman.

Scotty's Diner Owner: Scotty Blast and wife Gina, Lauren is waitress

Holiday Hair Salon

The house has been a hangout for many kids that have aided in our social experiment, making it way more fun and lively:

Bexley Vocal Ensemble
Mosaic School
Bexley Band
Bexley Young Life
Motherfolk - Epic Graduation party

Clubhouse – For Showing Up with Goal Setting and Music and an epic graduation party: Max Reichert, Ari & Zak Blumer, Ben Saulnier and Michael Berthold

The Bexley Men's Soccer Team for giving me courage to write my first book and allow me the honor of asking them to Show Up. This could not have happened without the faith of Coach Greg Kullman – who believes in goal setting and impacting the future through mentorship. Jacob Cini, Jordan Hoffman, Tucker Stas, Jacob Hodge, Will Gingery, Sam Addison, Sebstian Parra-Maya, Eli Feuer, Madrid Garcia, Adam Hirsh, Alex Eikenberry, Carl Pohlman, Mica Linger, Cody Philips, Max Fournier, Noah Appelbaum, Raphael Quastler, Jared James, Nate Meizlish, Daniel Loeser, Cole Heilman & Gray Levine

Mosaic Design Studio – Without the Team and our clients I would have never had the courage to help others in a global way.

Strategic Coach and Dan Sullivan

Kim White – My Angel

Kute Blackson to help me see that this is more than a personal story or book, it's a movement.

SWD (my brothers from another mother) for believing in my crazy dreams and always supporting me: Tom Hastings, Jason Pitstick, Jeff Burt, Mark Pottschmidt, Don Kenney, David Reim, Brian Reed, Daron Greene, Bill Kiefaber & Rob Lydic.

Supper Club (my sisters from another mother) for creating the sisterhood of entrepreneurship and support. Cookie McIntyre, Sandy Fekete, Jeanie Patrick, Sally Hughes, Kara Trott, Shelly Shively, Joelle Brock, Ann Rogers, Susan Eichinger, Kathy Eschelman, Cynthia Englefield, Sheri Tackett and Tara Abraham

All my Family:

Matt Miller, Linda Miller, Malloree Miller, Macee Miller, Jim Miller, (Little) Matt Miller, Renee Touris, Kelly Seeberg, Lori Allen, Andy Allen, AJ Allen, Annie Allen, Johny Allen, Lynn Starmer, Robert Starmer, Joey Cetrone, Sherry Cini-Putnam, Julie Cini, Sydney Jones, Cody Dieffenbaugher, Irene Vinton, Patty Berkebile, Jeff Berkebile, Maddie Berkebile, Patton Berkebile, Jerry Wilson, Patty Schario Milford, Jill & Jack, Matt & Jenna, Ben and Abby Diamond, Kris Putnam-Walkerly, Terry Walkerly & Austin & Isabella, Patty Milford, Glen Miller, Bonnie & Don Reed, Marilyn Johnson, The Keefers, The Gattusos, The Cugini's, The Milfords, The Blairs, The Reeds, The Millers, The Decosmos, The Boleys, The Lillys, The Tschudys and John and Linda Lilly. If I have forgotten someone please forgive me ☺

Mix Palmier for sharing his story and proving family is more than blood.

Timmy and Kathy Schapiro for encouraging me on my other book *The Future is Here... Senior Living Reimagined*

Special thanks to Nancy Greystone, without you this would still be a "project". I am forever grateful for your enthusiasm, accountability, brilliance, wit, collaboration and teamwork. I can't think of a better person to help me take my words and craft them so that they become a visual journey that encourages others in their social experiment creating a thriving hive.

Mom...let's face it, without what you do for Grandma there would be no Hive, you are the epicenter, self-sacrificing and ever evolving towards your best you. Grandma is blessed to have you as we all are. I love you to the moon and back. You have set the standard so high, it will be a challenge to come close.

Dad… you just roll with it all providing humor and safety. You make it look easy living with 4 generations of females. You're the best dad & grandfather.

Greg… my bird feeder, groundhog hunter, head construction worker, bee keeper, chicken farmer, rabbit caretaker, and all around good guy. I could probably rent you out as the best son-in-law in the world. Words can't express my thanks for all you have done for my grandmother and Parents. You not only provided the sweat for this experiment but are always thinking of unique cool ways to engage everyone. I love you…

Jacob… you gave up your room but never your love. Thank you for lighting up the house and every conversation with your positive energy. I can honestly say I have never seen you hold a grudge or wish I'll on others. You honor Matt in all you do. Thank you also for being the creative director for the book cover.

Adellina… my baby girl, I don't know many girl teenagers that were asked to live with a Great Grandmother and Grandparents. Everyone always counted on you to fill in when and where grandma needed and you always rose to the occasion, from great grandma sitting to cooking and cleaning. You love your old people and honor them with all you do. Thank you for also formatting the floor plans for the book and more.

Printed in the United States
By Bookmasters